YEAR A
AFTER PENTECOST 1

YEAR A
AFTER PENTECOST 1

PREACHING THE REVISED COMMON LECTIONARY

Marion Soards
Thomas Dozeman
Kendall McCabe

ABINGDON PRESS
Nashville

PREACHING THE REVISED COMMON LECTIONARY
YEAR A: AFTER PENTECOST 1

This book is printed on recycled, acid-free paper.

Library of Congress Cataloging-in-Publication Data

Soards, Marion L., 1952–
Preaching the revised Common lectionary.

Includes indexes.
[1] Advent, Christmas, Epiphany— [2] Lent and Easter.— [3] After Pentecost 1.
1. Bible—Liturgical lessons, English. 2. Bible —Homiletical use. I. Dozeman, Thomas B. II. McCabe, Kendall, 1939– . III. Title.
BS391.2.S59 1992 251 91-34039
ISBN 0-687-33872-7

93 94 95 96 97 98 99 00 01 — 10 9 8 7 6 5 4 3

MANUFACTURED IN THE UNITED STATES OF AMERICA

Contents

Introduction

Now pastors and students have a systematic treatment of essential issues of the Christian year and Bible study for worship and proclamation based on the Revised Common Lectionary. Interpretation of the lectionary will separate into three parts: Calendar, Canon, and Celebration. A brief word of introduction will provide helpful guidelines for utilizing this resource in worship through the Christian year.

Calendar. Every season of the Christian year will be introduced with a theological interpretation of its meaning, and how it relates to the overall Christian year. This section will also include specific liturgical suggestions for the season.

Canon. The lectionary passages will be interpreted in terms of their setting, structure, and significance. First, the word *setting* is being used loosely in this commentary to include a range of different contexts in which biblical texts can be interpreted from literary setting to historical or cultic settings. Second, regardless of how the text is approached under the heading of setting, interpretation will always proceed to an analysis of the structure of the text under study. Third, under the heading of significance, central themes and motifs of the passage will be underscored to provide a theological interpretation of the text as a springboard for preaching. Thus interpretation of the lectionary passages will result in the outline on the next page.

Celebration. This section will focus on specific ways of relating the lessons to liturgical acts and/or homiletical options for the day on which they occur. How the texts have been used in the Christian tradition will sometimes be illustrated to stimulate the thinking of preachers and planners of worship services.

I. OLD TESTAMENT TEXTS

A. The Old Testament Lesson

1. Setting

2. Structure

3. Significance

B. Psalm

1. Setting

2. Structure

3. Significance

II. NEW TESTAMENT TEXTS

A. The Epistle

1. Setting

2. Structure

3. Significance

B. The Gospel

1. Setting

2. Structure

3. Significance

Why We Use the Lectionary

Although many denominations have been officially or unofficially using some form of the lectionary for many years some pastors are still unclear about where it comes from, why some lectionaries differ from denomination to denomination, and why the use of a lectionary is to be preferred to a more random sampling of scripture.

Simply put, the use of a lectionary provides a more diverse scriptural diet for God's people, and it can help protect the congregation from the whims and prejudices of the pastor and other worship planners. Faithful use of the lectionary means that preachers must deal with texts they would rather ignore, but about which the congregation may have great concern and interest. God's command to Abraham to sacrifice his son Isaac, which we encounter in this volume, might be a case in point. Adherence to the lectionary can be an antidote to that homiletical arrogance that says, "I know what my people need," and in humility acknowledges that the Word of God found in scripture may speak to more needs on Sunday morning than we even know exist, when we seek to proclaim faithfully the message we have wrestled from the text.

The lectionary may also serve as a resource for liturgical content. The psalm is intended to be a response to the Old Testament lesson, and not read as a lesson itself, but beyond that the lessons may inform the content of prayers of confession, intercession, and petition. Some lessons may be adapted as affirmations of faith, as in *The United Methodist Hymnal,* nos. 887-889; the United Church of Christ's *Hymnal,* nos. 429-430; and the Presbyterian *Worshipbook,* no. 30. The "Celebration" entries for each day will call attention to these opportunities from time to time.

Pastors and preachers in the free-church tradition should think of the lectionary as a primary resource for preaching and worship, but need to remember that the lectionary was made for them and not they for the lectionary. The lectionary may serve as the inspiration for a separate series of lessons and sermons that will include texts not in the present edition, or having chosen one of the lectionary passages as the basis for the day's sermon, the preacher may wish to make an independent choice of the other lessons to supplement and illustrate the primary text. The lectionary will be of most value when its use is not a cause for legalism but for inspiration.

Just as there are no perfect preachers, there are no perfect lectionaries. The Revised Common Lectionary, upon which this series is based, is the result of the work of many years by the Consultation on Common Texts and is a response to ongoing evaluation of the *Common Lectionary* (1983) by pastors and scholars from the several participating denominations. The current interest in the lectionary can be traced back to the Second Vatican Council, which ordered lectionary revision for the Roman Catholic Church:

> The treasures of the Bible are to be opened up more lavishly, so that richer fare may be provided for the faithful at the table of God's Word. In this way a more representative portion of the holy Scriptures will be read to the people over a set cycle of years. (*The Documents of Vatican II*, Walter Abbott, ed. [Piscataway, N.J.: New Century, 1974], p. 155)

The example thus set by Roman Catholics inspired Protestants to take more seriously the place of the Bible in their services and sermons, and soon many denominations had issued their own three-year cycles, based generally on the Roman Catholic model but with their own modifications. This explains why some discrepancies and variations appear in different forms of the lectionary. The Revised Common Lectionary (RCL) is an effort to increase agreement among the churches. A table at the end of the volume will list the differences between the RCL and the Roman Catholic, Episcopal, and Lutheran lectionaries. Where no entry is made, all are in agreement with the RCL.

For those unacquainted with the general pattern of the lectionary, a brief word of explanation may be helpful for sermon preparation. (1) The three years are each distinguished by one of the Synoptic Gospels: Matthew in A, Mark in B, Luke in C. John is distributed over the three years with a heavy emphasis during Lent and Easter. (2) Two types of readings are used. During the periods of Advent to Epiphany and Lent to Pentecost, the readings are usually topical, that is, there is some common theme among them. During the Sundays after Epiphany and Pentecost the readings are continuous, with no necessary connection between the lessons. In the period covered by this volume, there is a thematic connection for Trinity Sunday, but the rest of the Sundays follow continuous Old Testament (Genesis and Exodus), epistle (Romans), and Gospel (Matthew) tracks. The Old Testament readings are from the Pentateuch in recognition of Matthew's concern to portray the church as the continuation of the sacred history which begins with God's promise to Abraham. In Romans we find Paul wrestling with the issue of the salvation of Israel in light of that original promise. These are bold, general themes, and are intended to provide a theological environment for homiletical thought rather than a thematic outline between all three lessons from week to week. Perhaps it should also be added that though the psalm is intended to be a response by the people to the Old Testament lesson—rather than as a lesson on its own—this in no way suggests that it cannot be used as the text for the sermon.

This is the third of four volumes that deal with the lessons for the entire A Cycle of the Christian year. Volume 2 includes Ash Wednesday through the Day of Pentecost. Volume 3 begins with Trinity Sunday (the First Sunday After Pentecost) and includes all the lessons for June, July, and August. Volume 4 finishes the remainder of the year, including the lessons for All Saints' Day (November 1) and Thanksgiving Day. A new series will then be published for the B Cycle.

A note on language: We have used the term *Old Testament* in this series because that is the language employed by the Consultation on Common Texts, at least up to this point. Pastors and worship committees may wish to consider alternative terms, such as *First Testament* or *Hebrew Scriptures*, that do not imply that those writings somehow have less value than the rest of the Christian Bible. Another option is to refer to *First Lesson* (always from the Hebrew Scriptures), *Second Lesson* (from Acts or the epistles), and *Gospel.*

SUMMER SUNDAY PREACHING IN PENTECOST

Few preachers apparently look forward to that long expanse of Sundays reaching from Trinity Sunday to Labor Day. Summer is a time for planning what will happen after Labor Day, and for vacations. Father's Day, the Fourth, and Labor Day Sunday are not high holy days on the calendars of most local churches. At most, these events are blips on the liturgical screen. Indeed, two months intervene between Independence Day and Labor Day, and the preacher's imagination is taxed to find ways in which to make service and sermon "meaningful." This creative breakdown has been known to result in various kinds of experimental and innovative liturgies and sermons—which, if they fail, make no listener feel too badly, since they were in the nature of a trial balloon or an attention getter. They perhaps provide sufficient justification for defining liturgical reform as that which is intended to protect the people of God from the clever ideas of the leadership!

Into this dilemma comes the lectionary as a means of introducing what might seem to be a revolutionary concept in many places—reading, studying, and celebrating the scriptural witness in a consecutive way over a sustained period of time. The "consecutive" study and celebration of Scripture over a period of time will help the preacher appreciate and understand the overall structure of the lectionary.

During the "proper" times of the year, Advent to Epiphany and Ash Wednesday to Pentecost, the lessons are generally chosen so as to have some kind of thematic connection, drawing together varied scriptural witnesses to help us gain insight into the meaning of the sacred mystery being anticipated or celebrated. Volumes 1 and 2 in this series illustrate that pattern. Even the "ordinary" Sundays between Epiphany and Ash Wednesday have the Old Testament lessons chosen in relation to the day's Gospel which, with the epistle, is being read sequentially. But when we come to the ordinary time after Pentecost, the lessons operate on three independent tracks with no intentional thematic relationship between them.

In Year A, the ruling Gospel is Matthew, the Gospel that is greatly concerned with representing Jesus as the fulfillment of the messianic promise and the new Moses who on the mount proclaims a new law. Thus the Old Testament lessons after Pentecost are chosen from the Pentateuch to complement Matthew's interests. They begin with the promise to Abraham and Sarah and conclude with the death of the judge Sampson. The intent is not that there be a one-on-one thematic connection between the two readings, but rather that the Old Testament lessons provide us with the context and tradition within which Matthew was thinking and writing. The epistle texts throughout the summer months are from Romans, a volume in which Paul depends heavily upon the Abraham and Sarah narratives as he develops his theology of grace.

The lectionary creators intend that the order of reading be Old Testament, psalm response, epistle, Gospel. The psalm is a response to the Old Testament lesson not a lesson in itself (though that does not mean it cannot be used as the text for the sermon, since it is a part of the canon). This use of the psalter as a resource for prayer and praise reminds us of our roots in synagogue and the Temple. In the epistle, we hear the apostolic witness, which understands itself to be in continuity with the work of God in the experience of Israel in the Old Testament and sees itself as a fulfillment of God's promise to Israel. The Gospel is read last, because that is the vehicle through which the community interprets both the experience of Israel and the primitive Church. There is a kind of historical development here, since usually each reading is older in time than the one following it, but this is no justification for the pattern. The rationale is unabashedly christological. It is through Christ that we view and interpret both the witness of the Old Testament and the apostles. It is for this reason that in many traditions the congregation stands to hear the Gospel read—not because the Gospels are somehow "better" Scripture, but because they are an icon of Christ in our midst, and it is Christ whom we stand to greet.

This means that the order of the texts is not changed so that the one with the primary text is closest to the sermon, because we still need the word of Christ through which to focus our attention. Even if, in ordinary time, the Gospel does not relate thematically to any of the previous readings it is still the last text because of the symbolic lesson to be learned. It may be that there is a particular Gospel text that the preacher has used as a vehicle for interpreting one of the earlier lessons. That may provide a justification for changing the Gospel of the day in order to establish the thematic connection. For example, Proper 13 has as the Old Testament lesson the story of Jacob wrestling with the angel. The Gospel is the story of the feeding of the five thousand in chapter 14, a rich mine for preaching, but which may be difficult to relate to Genesis 32! This preacher might exercise personal freedom to change the Gospel for the day to Matthew 26:36-46, describing Jesus' agony in the garden, for reasons that should be apparent to the homilitician. This decision maintains the priority of Matthew, and it allows for a closer analysis of one part of the Passion narrative, since in the lectionary it would only have appeared in the reading of the Passion narrative on Passion/Palm Sunday. The epistle for the day is Paul's wrestling with the question of Israel's salvation, which can certainly stand as a reading on its own, but may also provide an interpretive perspective for the other two lessons (particularly when joined with Charles Wesley's classic hymn on Genesis 32, "Come, O Thou Traveler Unknown").

This kind of creative and critical thinking allows for an expansion of the lectionary by the insightful preacher if each set is taken in turn each three years as the governing lesson and the preacher then makes other thematic choices (assuming that the integrity of the texts is maintained). Already one's preaching ministry has developed possibilities for the next nine years and brought into question the accusation that the lectionary limits the preacher's choice of texts.

In recent years, the dictum that the text and the sermon should not be separated has become a kind of mantra that has given rise to a new liturgical legalism, which does not understand the liturgical setting out of which the dictum originated. The reason for the rule is not to disallow a hymn between lesson and sermon (or even two lessons with responses). It grows out of the practice, still current in some places, of having the (one and only) Scripture lesson very early in the service, followed by a pastoral prayer, an anthem, the offering, the announcements, a hymn, special solo music, and whatever else, and then finally the sermon. The dictum is intended to prevent this kind of separation because it encourages the preacher to preach the Word, which is more likely not to happen when the Scripture is long forgotten after the beginning of the service.

Though it may be called "ordinary" time, it is still *kairos* with which we are dealing, and for the Christian time is always a vehicle for grace. Ideally, the lectionary creators intend that there be a convergence of the Word of the Lord with the Supper of the Lord on the Day of the Lord. The dismemberment of these elements in practice has led to a diminished identity on the part of the Christian community. The Word without the Supper becomes as breath without body, because it denies the incarnational principle enunciated in John 1, which is at the heart of the Christian revelation. No less tragic is the celebration of the Supper without the proclamation of the Word, which gives us a body without breath. And equally tragic is the confusion of the Sabbath with the Lord's Day. It is often easier to observe the Sabbath with its negations than to live with the scandalous joy and grace that characterize life in the Kingdom.

During ordinary time we are challenged by what to do with Easter, since it is responsible for the whole enterprise that is the Christian Church. Easter is the formative event for Christians, the eighth day of the new creation, the day that reminds us that we die, are buried, and then raised with Christ. As a result, our view of the world will henceforth be slightly skewed, since we are learning to look at life from the other side of the Resurrection. Proper time is rather straightforward as we hear again the ancient narratives, remember "the old, old story," and rejoice at our incorporation into the mighty acts of God. But ordinary time is no time to act as though all of that never happened! On the contrary, ordinary time is the setting for applying Easter to make life extraordinary. Romans can give us a model this summer (as can others of Paul's letters at other times). Paul's great theological treatise ends up as a study in ethics with that most significant "therefore" in Romans 12:1 (see the epistle for Proper 16). The question always before us during ordinary time is,

What do we do about Easter? The lessons suggest resources in our search for answers. A strictly Sabbatarian view of the day will incline us to legalism and social security in our ethics; the Lord who picks corn on the Sabbath will have something to say to us about the hungry multitudes as we break bread with him at Table (see Proper 13).

The former pattern for counting the days in the Christian year always spoke of days "After Pentecost" or "After Trinity," and the tendency then was to think of that time as "the season of Pentecost." Both lectionary and calendar reform have recovered the primitive understanding that the Day of Pentecost is part of Easter, the Great Fifty Days, and that resurrection and empowerment by the Spirit are inseparable (see commentary in Year A, Lent and Easter of this series). We live empowered by the Spirit of the risen Christ, and "therefore," as Paul says, we are now about the business of seeking the things that are above, which has implications for how we go about the business of living here below. The preacher's exciting challenge this and every summer is to engage the congregation in dialogue about what it means to love God and do as you please!

The standard color for ordinary time is green. To avoid tedium and monotony during these six months, a variety of greens and summer colors might be used along with fresh flowers from local gardens. The readings for the day may also present ideas for different kinds of visuals from Sunday to Sunday.

Trinity Sunday (First Sunday After Pentecost)

Old Testament Texts

The two Old Testament texts for Trinity Sunday focus on the creative power of God, and, as such, they provide commentary on the Gospel lesson, where Jesus proclaims to his disciples in Matthew 28:18 that "all authority in heaven and on earth" has been given to him. Genesis 1:1–2:4*a* is the sweeping account of creation of order from chaos. Psalm 8 is a hymn that celebrates the creative power of God. Taken together these texts provide the vast stage upon which we must interpret this final saying of Jesus in the Gospel of Matthew.

The Lesson: *Genesis 1:1–2:4*a

Creation and Chaos

Setting. Creation mythologies are common throughout the ancient Near East. The words *creation* and *mythology* require a brief definition to provide the proper background for interpreting Genesis 1. First, *mythology* in the context of the ancient Near East means something that is ultimately true. From this starting point we would say that the story of Jesus is mythological because the account of his life goes beyond a three-year sequence of historical events and actually becomes a description of all of reality. This meaning runs against our current usage, where *myth* frequently means just the opposite, that something is "false," as in the statement, "That's a myth!" We frequently use this word pejoratively when someone lies or when a statement is not factual. Second, creation is the preferred genre in the ancient Near East for addressing the ultimate questions about the world that are the subject matter of mythology. Creation mythologies, therefore, are profoundly theological, for they always address at least the following four questions: (1) Who is God? (2) What is the nature of this world? (3) What is the relationship between God and this world? and (4) Who are we? or What does it mean to be human in the larger context of God's relationship to this world? All of these questions are central to Genesis 1, yet our interpretation will be limited to the first three. Psalm 8 will address the fourth question.

Structure. Genesis 1:1–2:4*a* is a rhythmic and repetitive text, which uses many stereotyped phrases in describing six days of creation. A number of scholars have observed that the rhythmic language results in the following five-part pattern for each day of creation: (1) Introduction: "And God said"; (2) Command: "Let there be"; (3) Completion: "And it was so"; (4) Judgment: "And God saw that it was good"; (5) Time Sequence: "And it was evening." The six days of creation are structured into yet another harmonious balance in which the last three days of creation build off the first three in the following manner:

Day 1 Light	Day 4 Luminaries
Day 2 Sky	Day 5 Birds/Fishes
Day 3 Land/Plants	Day 6 Animals/Humans

The six days of creation are also framed by an introduction and a conclusion, which present a stark contrast between chaos in 1:1-2 and God at rest in 2:1-4*a*, which results in the following outline:

I. Introduction (1:1-2): Description of Uncreated Chaos
II. Six days of Creation (1:3-31): Structuring of Chaos
III. Conclusion (2:1-4*a*): Description of God at Rest

Significance. Two concerns are important for preaching this text. The first is how the creation story in Genesis 1 answers the three questions of mythology that were listed above—namely, Who is God?, What is the world? and, What is God's relationship with the world? A brief look at the introduction and conclusion to Genesis 1:1–2:4*a* will provide a framework for answering these questions. The second issue is whether it is possible to preach a sermon on the Trinity from an Old Testament text like Genesis 1? Can we really talk about Jesus and the Holy Spirit in the narrow context of the first creation story? An examination of the role of Genesis 1:1–2:4*a* in the larger context of Scripture will provide guidelines of how we claim this text on Trinity Sunday.

First, what then does Genesis 1 say about God and creation? The introduction in 1:1-2 provides important information for answering this question, for it describes reality prior to God's creative activity, which begins with light in v. 3. Verse 1 attributes the creation of the heavens and the earth to God alone. The verb "to create" in v. 1 is only used with God as its subject. Thus v. 1 sets the tone for the entire account of creation, which has prompted scholars to describe this verse as a title for the whole piece. Verse 2 shifts the focus momentarily from God to a description of earth prior to the creative activity of God. Verse 2, therefore, is best interpreted as a snapshot of uncreated chaos, which, from the imagery of the verse, might be characterized as an enormous oil slick: It is formless, dark, and wet. Furthermore, the Hebrew words for "darkness" and "deep" invite the interpreter to see personality in the chaotic oil slick, for these words suggest cosmic powers from other ancient Near Eastern creation mythologies like the Babylonian *Enuma Elish*. These allusions to personality suggest that the subsequent divine acts of creation will not simply be a mopping up of an inanimate oil slick, but that the six days of creation (or the imposition of structure) are actually a limitation of a certain kind of power in the universe—the power of chaos. These opening verses say a great deal about God and creation. Verse 1 is a strong, unequivocal proclamation about the power of God to create. Then v. 2 makes it clear that the power to create is not effortless. The presence of chaos in this verse underscores two things: that there is resistance to God's structuring of a good creation—there is real evil in the world; and that creation is itself an act of divine grace—we don't fashion creation it is given to us. Finally the picture of the deity at rest in 2:1-4*a* demonstrates that God is an able creator who is capable of overcoming any resistance.

Second, is it possible to preach from Genesis 1:1–2:4*a* on Trinity Sunday? Verse 2 makes reference to the "spirit of God" moving over the face of the waters. Frequently this reference is equated with the

Holy Spirit, hence the use of this text on Trinity Sunday to anchor the Godhead in the origins of creation. Such a direct and anachronistic reading of Trinitarian theology presents problems because the "spirit of God" in v. 2 is a much more ambiguous concept in the Old Testament than the third person of the Trinity in Christian theology. In fact, the phrase may simply mean "mighty wind" in this context. Thus if we are focusing only on the imagery and language in Genesis 1 and trying to read more recent understandings of God back into the Old Testament, then we must conclude that it cannot be used as a Trinitarian text, for even if we identified the "spirit of God" with the Holy Spirit, we would still have to find Jesus someplace in the text to fill out our Trinity.

If the question is posed somewhat differently, however, from the perspective of what the Trinity actually means for Christians concerning Who God is? and What this world is?, then Genesis 1 becomes a powerful Trinitarian text. By confessing God as Trinity, we celebrate God as being the original Creator of this world (Father), its Savior (Son), and the One who continues to sustain it through time and brings it to its fulfillment (Holy Spirit). A confession of God as Trinity, therefore, requires a large vision of God and God's relationship to creation—not only as the Originator of the world, nor even simply as its Savior, but also as the one who brings it to its end. This large vision of God in relationship to creation through time allows us to read Genesis 1 on a much larger scale. We frequently interpret Genesis 1 only as an account of the origin of the world, and thus try to locate the Holy Spirit at that point. Genesis 1, however, has a much larger role in Scripture than simply providing an account of origins, for it is as much a vision of the end of the world as it is of its beginning. In many ways, the history of salvation story that is woven through Scripture (from the call of Abraham to the ministry of Jesus) is really an attempt to get back to the first chapter of Genesis. Biblical scholars describe this kind of linking of the origin and end of creation as being *urzeit* (primeval time) and *endzeit* (end time or eschatology). When we view Genesis 1 as having this larger role throughout Scripture, as both beginning and end, then it becomes a profoundly Trinitarian text, for it provides us with a glimpse of the end, which presupposes the full range of God's power as Creator, Savior, and

Sustainer. The creator God at rest, who has successfully restructured chaos, goes to the heart of what it means to confess God as Father, Son, and Holy Spirit, and it also provides the context for interpreting Jesus' post-Easter proclamation "that all power in heaven and on earth" is now his, for this statement is really about the power of God as Trinity—as Creator and Sustainer, as well as Savior.

The Response: *Psalm 8*

What Are Humans?

Setting. Psalm 8 is a hymn of praise that modulates between an individual voice (vv. 1*b*-8) and a community refrain (1*b*, 9). The central motif of the community refrain is the celebration of the name of God, which accounts for the inclusion of this psalm on this Sunday.

Structure. Psalm 8 separates into two sections: vv. 1-4 and 5-9. The community refrain begins the first section (1*b*) and concludes the last section (v. 9), with the result that the praise of God's name throughout the earth frames the entire psalm. The voice of the individual singer takes up the middle portion of the psalm. Within this section, the central theme of the psalm appears to be the question of v. 4: "What are human beings that you are mindful of them?" Most commentators agree that this question and the description of the role of humans in creation that follows in vv. 6-8 is based on the account of creation of humans in Genesis 1:26. Thus Psalm 8 should be read as inner-biblical reflection of Genesis 1.

Significance. Psalm 8 is somewhat unusual in that it is a hymn of praise that addresses God in the second person ("you"). The use of the second person establishes a certain intimacy in the relationship between the singer and God, which is striking because it contrasts with the vast (and impersonal) creation imagery that is the subject matter of much of the hymn (God is sovereign; majestic; creator of heavens, moon, and stars; and so on). This contrast between the intimate relationship of singer and God on the one hand, and the vastness of the creation order on the other is an important point of entry into interpreting Psalm 8, for it provides the background for the central question in v. 4: What are humans to God in the larger context of the universe? On such a larger stage our first response would be that humans are insignificant in the larger drama of creation. Psalm 8 is a hymn of praise because just the opposite is true. God is not only mindful of earth-bound mortals (v. 4), but he has even given them a formative role as actors on the large stage of creation. One suspects that this paradox—between the insignificance of humans in the larger context of creation and the degree of attention that God bestows on them—may provide insight for interpreting v. 2, which has no parallel any place in Scripture. Perhaps it is the frail human mortals who are the babes of v. 2 that God has chosen as a defense against evil, even though God had so many more resources at his disposal ("You have set your glory above the heavens.") This fact is then what prompts the wonder and awe of the psalmist concerning the position of humans in the larger drama of God's creation.

New Testament Texts

The lectionary brings together two quite distinct passages in the lessons for this Sunday. But at a glance anyone can see that these texts were selected because they contain Trinitarian language in seemingly polished formal statements. Either lesson or both lessons provide(s) scriptural precedent for reflection on the doctrine of the Trinity, but neither text is actually an expression of fully formulated Trinitarian thought, as is clear from reading the entire books in which these passages occur.

The Epistle: *II Corinthians 13:11-13 (14)*

Appealing to and Blessing the Congregation

Setting. The problem Paul confronts in II Corinthians is a controversy caused by certain self-professed Christian preachers who have come among the Corinthians with boldness. Paul refers to these opponents as "super-apostles," perhaps a sarcastic allusion from the apostle but possibly the self-designation of the super-apostles. The text of II Corinthians is difficult, containing several hard, if not impossible, transitions (see any standard commentary). The tones of the recognizable sections of the letter vary; Paul is sometimes conciliatory, sometimes defensive, sometimes laudatory, and sometimes fiercely pugnacious. The verses in this lesson conclude the final section of the letter (chapters 10-13), which is by far the most combative part of the epistle.

Structure. II Corinthians 13 falls into two main parts: vv. 1-10 are Paul's final warning and admonitions to the Corinthians, and vv. 11-14 formally close the letter. The first unit, vv. 1-10, has two sub-sections. Verses 1-4 inform the Corinthians that Paul is about to pay them a visit and warns them to make sure they are ready. These verses set the subsequent material in context, including our lesson. Verses 5-10 issue an appeal and plainly state Paul's purpose for writing.

The actual lesson for today, vv. 11-14, may cause a slight problem, because some English language Bibles versify these lines 13:10-14 (e.g., KJV) while others mark the text with vv. 10-13 (e.g., NRSV). It is not that some translations have an additional verse, but that some divide v. 12 in Greek into two parts in English, vv. 12-13. The motivation for shifting this section from three to four verses is superstition—namely, a desire to avoid ending this letter with verse 13:13. Critical editions of the Greek text versify 13:10-13.

Significance. Near the beginning of the chapter (vv. 3*b*-4), Paul makes his argument both relevant and christological by maintaining the christological paradox of weakness and power. The idea of divine power perfected in weakness comes from the heart of Paul's theology. It is a striking and difficult concept, but in essence Paul believes that his human weakness serves as a conduit for the very power of God into the real world. Paul may mean that as he has suffered the Corinthians' foolishness in his weakness (having been formerly shamed by their conduct). Now, because he did so, they shall experience the power of God confronting them as it will be manifested in Paul's presence. At root Paul's conviction is that the sovereignty of God cannot be thwarted, though the Corinthians may attempt to resist or reject it.

Paul appeals for the Corinthians to examine their life as a church and to straighten up—the second person language is plural here. The reason Paul gives for the Corinthians' auditing and altering their congregational existence is purely christological: Christ is in/among them. Paul's own desire for the Corinthians is clearly stated in verses 9*b*-10, but translations generally miss the sense of the statement. The word translated "perfection," "improvement," or "perfect" (*katartisis*) in 13:9*b* was originally a medical term for setting bones, so that Paul longs for the correction of what is fractured in Corinth. Paul calls for repair work to be done! This insight into the text may help us know how to employ this lesson for preaching.

The letter concludes in three moves in verses 11-13 [14]—our reading for today. Paul issues final admonitions, exchanges greetings, and pronounces a lofty benediction. Verse 11 reiterates Paul's essential advice and plainly theologizes the directions with a kind of blessing. The power to face their problems and work the necessary changes for which Paul calls will not simply come from the Corinthians. It will ultimately come from God, and Paul recognizes that crucial fact here. Verse 12 may cause us a few problems, especially if we try to follow the apostle's advice; for we do not know exactly what the "holy kiss" was. Speculating on the meaning is no solution to our ignorance, and experimenting won't guarantee we'll find the truth! Perhaps this verse can best remind us that there are some things we don't know! What we can know about the holy kiss is that it is holy because it was passed among the holy ones or saints who have been made holy by the reconciling work of God in Christ. Not the act, but the God-created context of the Church makes this enigmatic kiss sacred.

Finally, for Trinity Sunday, we come to the very stylized benediction. Some regard this as the earliest Trinitarian formulation, but such an interpretation is beyond the sense of the Pauline text in its historical context. But this negative historical conclusion won't preach! Nor should it! Notice these items in relation to this verse: First, the order is striking. Paul mentions, in turn, the Lord Jesus Christ, God, and the Holy Spirit. From texts like I Corinthians 15 we know that Paul has a notion of ultimate christological subjugation, but for the present, God's work is being advanced by the risen and exalted Lord Jesus. In the context of Paul's full range of statements about God, Christ, and the Spirit, we find no developed doctrine of the Trinity; here he is actually declaring the grace and love of God in God's dealings with the Corinthians, and he is declaring that their own existence, fellowship, and participation is in a God-created context.

A sermon could be developed from Paul's appeals and reasoning in the larger passage in which the verses of our lesson occur and, then, worship could conclude with the pronouncement of this benediction. Or, should one concentrate on the Trinity in the sermon, verse 13 [14] could be a point of departure for a didactic sermon that will move beyond the text but show the anchoring of later Christian reflection in the biblical waters of this passage.

The Gospel: *Matthew 28:16-20*

The Who, What, and How of Discipleship

Setting. Matthew tells the story of Jesus' Passion in a manner similar to the other Gospels, but there is a distinctive point of view on the events, and there is additional information found only in Matthew's story. The Resurrection account is similar to the stories found in Luke and John, but here there is a high percentage of material found only in Matthew. The ending of the gospel according to Matthew (the lesson for this Sunday) is part of Matthew's unique material. We find the disciples on a mountain in Galilee with the risen Jesus.

Structure. Verses 16-17 open the scene and locate the disciples in time, place, and mood. Verses 18-20 are a pronouncement by Jesus in three evolving parts: a declaration of Jesus' authority (18*b*), a commissioning of the disciples (19-20*a*), and a reminder that issues a promise (20*b*).

Significance. This closing scene of Matthew is set on a mountain in Galilee. A specific identification is not important, for this mountain functions more symbolically than literally. Throughout Matthew one encounters Jesus and his disciples on mountains: Jesus (without the disciples) is tempted by Satan on a mountain (4:8); Jesus speaks his most famous sermon on a mountain (5:1); Jesus goes off alone to pray on a mountain (14:23); Jesus does miraculous healing as he sits on a mountain (15:29); the Transfiguration of Jesus occurs on a high mountain (17:1)—and now the ending comes on a mountain. The mountain motif in Matthew conjures up our memory of Old Testament mountains that were places of divine work and revelation, so the mention of a mountain here creates a level of expectation.

The strange note about the reaction of the disciples is probably an editorial device to create an ideal sense of a historical reality, namely that there was a mixture of reactions among the disciples to the Resurrection with some doubt mixed into the worship. Matthew does no more than recognize and recall this phenomenon. His candor may help us use this powerful story in our own preaching, for the mood in congregations today is usually not different from the disposition Matthew attributes to the disciples—genuine reverence is laced with troubling doubts. Notice that Christ issues no rebuke.

As a risen Jesus comes to the disciples, he speaks words that emphasize the meaning of the present exaltation of Christ for discipleship. The combined statements (declaration, commission, reminder-promise) have the force of comforting the disciples—some of whom have lingering doubts. The statement about Christ's authority employs the passive form, stating subtly that God has empowered Jesus to empower others. Acting on his authority, Jesus directs the disciples into mission ("therefore," 28:19). The mission is the making of disciples through the activities of baptizing and teaching. The sequence in this direction recognizes that the work of making disciples is ultimately the work of the risen Christ and God. The activities—baptizing and teaching—revse a "conversion" logic that would have the disciples teaching so as to persuade others who would, in turn, be baptized. In Matthew's theology, Christians become disciples through baptism; and they are disciples by doing what Jesus commands, that is what he taught. The last part of the risen Jesus' words reminds the disciples of his promised eternal presence. This Gospel opens with the angel calling the child "Emmanuel," or "God with us"; and now at the end Jesus, authorized by God, promises constant and eternal presence. The disciples are to work with Jesus, not merely for him.

This text names the Trinity in the reference to baptism (28:19). Again, this is not a fully developed concept, which a reading of Matthew shows. Remarkably the version of this text cited by Eusebius (*Ecclesiastical History* III.5.2) prior to the Council of Nicea had the words "in my name" instead of "baptizing them in the name of the Father and of the Son and of the Holy Spirit"; so that it is not impossible that the earliest version of this tradition did not contain this formula—although there is no serious textual evidence to support this reading for Matthew. Thus what can this formula mean in Matthew? Since Matthew understands Christianity to be living the words of the earthly Jesus by/in the power and the presence of the risen Lord Jesus, these words may simply mean that as God sent Jesus, now God sends the Holy Spirit (the spirit of the risen Jesus) to direct and comfort faithful disciples.

Trinity Sunday: The Celebration

Ordinary time is always bracketed by special days, whether after Epiphany or Pentecost. After Epiphany the days are the Baptism of the Lord and the Transfiguration. After Pentecost they are Trinity Sunday and Christ the King.

Trinity Sunday represents a summing up of the divine activity that we have been celebrating since the beginning of Advent. It also suggests a reminder of the whole work and being of God in creation, redemption, and sanctification, which is still ongoing and provides the context for our life of celebration and witness throughout the rest of ordinary time.

Today is also a celebration of Sunday, the Lord's Day, as distinct from the Sabbath, so it can be an opportunity to reinforce what is meant by the sanctification of time, the use of time as a means of remembering what God has done. The hymn, "O Day of Rest of Gladness," makes the Trinitarian connection explicitly and so is most appropriate as the opening hymn on this day:

On you, at earth's creation,
  The light first had its birth;
On you, for our salvation,
  Christ rose from depths of earth;
On you, our Lord victorious
  The Spirit sent from heaven;
And thus on you, most glorious,
  A threefold light was given.

Having said so much about the action of the Trinity, it is perhaps more important to stress the being of the Trinity in order to avoid some kind of functionalist heresy. What the Church is involved in on this day is the praise of God for being God—no more and no less. This can be a day for the liturgy and the sermon to help people rediscover the mystery of the faith and to adore the mystery of God for its own sake. This is no time for a theological treatise; it is time to be "lost in wonder, love, and praise."

A discussion of the Trinity in terms of being can help diffuse much of the controversy surrounding language, since it will make clear the inadequacy of any language to describe God. Thoughtful consideration of the topic can help open the way to the use of alternate images that can expand our appreciation of what may have been originally intended but is now obscured by the traditional Trinitarian language. Augustine's understanding of the Trinity as a trinity of love, each part participating fully in the life of the other parts so that they are indistinguishable, commends much sanity and charity in the contemporary debate. Today the Church celebrates the mystery of love, not a problem in mathematics.

Proper Six
Sunday Between June 12 and 18 Inclusive (If After Trinity Sunday)

Old Testament Texts

The Old Testament texts for this Sunday explore the question of whether anything is too difficult for God. This question is central to the story of Sarah's miraculous birth in Genesis 18:1-15; 21:1-7, while Psalm 116:1-2, 12-19 is a song of thanksgiving, which celebrates the fact that indeed nothing is beyond God's reach.

The Lesson: *Genesis 18:1-15 (21:1-7)*

Is Anything Too Difficult for God?

Setting. The Old Testament lesson for this Sunday is a familiar miracle story about the birth of Isaac. Nevertheless, its setting in the larger context of the book of Genesis may help to see more clearly how this is a story about God and Sarah, which focuses on the question of whether God is reliable. The promise of an heir frames the ancestral stories in Genesis. It is introduced in Genesis 12:1-4 and remains the central organizing theme throughout Genesis. The Old Testament lesson for this Sunday must be read in the light of this larger promise of God, for the advanced age of Abraham and Sarah call into question God's reliability. Furthermore, as we will see more clearly in the section on Significance, this is not a story about Abraham, rather it is a story about Sarah, which sketches first her private unbelief, its unmasking by God, and finally her affirmation of God's miracle in the birth of Isaac. The transformations that take place in Sarah provide the setting for her final words in 21:6-7, which provide us with an answer to the question of whether anything is too difficult for God.

Structure. Genesis 18:1-15 (and 21:1-7) can be read very easily as a single story, which separates into two main sections, each of which subdivides further into two smaller episodes. The first section is an introduction for the main story of Sarah and God, which takes place in the second section.

- I. Introduction (18:1-10*a*)
  - A. Initial meeting (vv. 1-5)
    - 1. Setting (vv. 1-2)
    - 2. Speech (vv. 3-5)
  - B. Meal
    - 1. Setting (vv. 6-8)
    - 2. Speech (vv. 9-10*a*)
- II. The Miracle Story of Isaac's Birth (18:10*b*-15; 21:1-7)
  - A. Divine promise of a miraculous birth and Sarah's unbelief (vv. 10*b*-15)
    - 1. Setting (vv. 10*b*-11)
    - 2. Speech (vv. 12-15)
  - B. The Miraculous birth and Sarah's belief
    - 1. Setting (21:1-5)
    - 2. Speech (21:6-7)

Significance. Notice how the story is structured to alternate between a narrative that provides a setting for speeches and the actual discourse by different characters. It is the speeches that carry the message of the story, especially the speeches between Sarah and God in the second part. The introduction in 18:1-10*a* provides a setting for Sarah to take center stage. In the initial meeting at the door of the tent in 18:1-5, Abraham is not even named. His function in this story is to recognize the divine status of the three guests and to invite them to dinner, which provides transition to Sarah since she prepares a meal for the three divine guests. The centrality of Sarah to this story is confirmed when the three guests initiate speech at the close of the meal in vv. 9-10*a*. Abraham is not the object of their interests; rather it is Sarah, and they ask where she is and then state that she will become pregnant and have a child in the Spring. The speech by the three divine guests (who then become God in v. 10*a*) closes the introduction.

The central section of the story consists of Genesis 18:10*b*-15 and 21:1-7. The first of the two episodes begins in v. 10*b*-11 by locating Sarah and thus providing a setting for her speech. We learn that she was listening, that she is alone, and that she is well past menopause. A complex sequence of speeches follows. First, Sarah demonstrates her unbelief by laughing privately over this seemingly ridiculous promise in v. 12. The motif of laughing remains central to the rest of the story because in Hebrew it is the name of Isaac. Second, God asks Abraham in vv. 13-14 why Sarah is laughing and then poses the central question to the story: Is there anything that is too difficult for God? The Hebrew could just as well read: Is there any miracle that God cannot perform? Third, Sarah, who has been secretly listening, now realizes that her unbelief has been unmasked, so she lies in v. 15, which doesn't impress God. The story ends in 21:1-7. Verses 1-5 provide a new setting. We learn that a child was indeed born and that he was named Isaac (laughter). The new setting creates the context for one last discourse, which of course must be from Sarah, since this is really her story. Like her first speech in v. 12, she once again appears to be alone, but her discourse is no longer a private rumination. Instead it seems to be directed outward to any one who may care to listen to her, and she has two things to say. First, she states that she is the object of her own joke by punning on the word laughter, for her laughter of disbelief is now laughter of belief as she breast-feeds an infant named Laughter (Isaac). Second, she ends her speech with a rhetorical question, which would appear to require an answer from us, the readers of her story: Who would have thought that God could produce such a miraculous birth?

The Response: *Psalm 116:1-2, 12-19*

Giving God the Thanks

Setting. Psalm 116:1-2, 12-19 is a thanksgiving song of the individual. Such songs recount a past crisis, but from the experience of having been rescued. The song, therefore, is meant to recount

God's salvation of the one singing, but it is directed to the whole community of faith, which is invited to join in the celebration.

Structure. In some versions, Psalm 116:1-9 is a separate psalm from vv. 10-19, although it is not in the Masoretic text. The entire psalm can be outlined in the following manner:

I. The Introit (vv. 1-2)
II. A Description of Past Crisis (vv. 3-4)
III. Praise to God for Present Salvation (vv. 5-11)
IV. Vow to Praise (vv. 12-19)

Significance. The words of the psalmist, with their movement from past crisis to the present experience of salvation, could very well function as the words of Sarah at the end of her song. Furthermore, the setting of the individual song of thanksgiving, with its focus on the whole community of faith, also provides a parallel to the end of Sarah's story, where her final speech is really directed to the reader. Both the end of the story in Genesis 18:1-15; 21:1-7 and Psalm 116:1-2, 12-19 provide focus for preaching, because they invite the worshiping congregation to claim the transformation in the character of Sarah from unbelief to belief as affirmation of their own faith in God's ability to save.

New Testament Texts

As we move into ordinary time, we return to Romans and Matthew. The passages in the lessons for this and the following weeks are but selected sequential readings, so that whatever thematic correlations one perceives may be deliberate, accidental, or creatively imagined!

The Epistle: *Romans 5:1-8*

From Weakness to the Strength of Salvation

Setting. Romans 5:1-11 was the epistle reading for the third Sunday in Lent in Year A. The following commentary is in part a repetition of the entry for that Sunday.

The dominant concern of chapters 5–8 is the life of the Christian community, especially in its experience of grace. The foregoing chapters were concerned with the righteousness of God and the sin of humankind, Jews and Gentiles, law and faith; and these themes were developed through a series of exegetical arguments. A turn from theological juxtapositions and exegetical explanations began in 4:23-25, and now in chapter 5 we find Paul meditating overtly on the nature and significance of Christian existence in this world. The previous polemic and dialectic yields to a celebration of grace that is essentially straightforward.

Structure. The passage has two complementary parts. Verses 1-5 declare our (let us stand with the Romans and not at a distance) justification and expand upon that theme. Verses 6-8 elucidate the meaning of Jesus Christ's death for our lives.

Significance. One is sorely tempted to do a series of word studies in relation to this passage, since it is loaded with significant theological terminology. Such a tactic may unpack much of the meaning of this text, but it will also render Paul's thinking fairly static, whereas in fact he is expressing the dynamic quality of Christian life in these verses. Thus we need to create a sense of motion that will impart some of Paul's own energy to our congregations when reflecting on this passage.

Paul starts with the present, saying that we are justified by faith (literally, Paul speaks spatially, not instrumentally, saying "we are justified out of faith"). Being justified in theological terms is like being justified in typing or printing; it means that everything has been set into a proper line. Christians are neither ragged-right nor ragged-left, we are justified. Actually, we have been justified because God has set us into the right relationship with God's self through Jesus Christ. Thus, our justification is grace! This good news puts us at peace, because, Paul says, we have (through being justified) access to grace. But this experience of the goodness of God is neither static nor complete! For the apostle immediately talks of our hope. Hope is related to our future, which has been created by the gracious work of God in Jesus Christ. For Paul, this scheme is far from "possibility thinking"; rather, it is "reality living." So Paul continues his meditation by bringing us all down into the swamps of life—suffering. Yet look how Paul can speak of suffering. He does not deny its reality.

He does not glorify it. Instead he puts a good face on it by relating it to endurance and character-building. Oddly, the outcome of our suffering, which produces endurance and builds character, is that we hope.

Paul has taken us for a ride in a logical loop: We rejoice in our hope allowing us to rejoice in our suffering, which yields endurance and increases character and produces hope. Christian existence, created by grace, is set in motion after hope, which is not yet fully realized but which is already present in a preliminary way. Paul says we live as we do because God's own love is poured into our hearts by the Holy Spirit. Paul continues by speaking of our past. He says we were weak. By this he means that we were formerly ungodly, we were sinners, our lives were not lived in obedience to God's will. But perhaps because he has already devoted significant attention to our sinfulness (Romans 1:18–3:20), Paul does not ponder that matter here. Instead, with the time and space of our ungodly past evoked, Paul drops God's saving work in Jesus Christ into our midst. Then we move back to the present, and Paul once again declares our current status by saying that now we are justified by the death of Jesus Christ. The apostle is not interested in explaining how Christ's death justifies us; rather, he wishes to remark on the marvelously unmerited character of God's love. Though we did not deserve it, nevertheless God's love is so great that it did for us what we could not do for ourselves—it justified us!

A sermon could well begin with reflection on the marvelous character of God's unmerited saving love. From there it could move to consider "our reconciliation" (vv. 10-11), which is justification and hope. Perhaps this theme could be developed by reversing Paul's order. Speaking of our future in Christ can be made "real" by concluding with reflection on present Christian life as those who are justified. Being justified means that our lives have been set in line with the will of God, so that now we are set up by God to live in obedience to God's will.

The Gospel: *Matthew 9:35–10:8 (9-23)*

Calling and Training Shepherds

Setting. Matthew presents the account of Jesus' ministry (3:1–26:1*a*) in five recognizable sections, each ending with a version of the formula, "And when Jesus finished these sayings, . . ." The Gospel for this Sunday comes in the second major section, Matthew 8:1–11:1, which tells of the ministry in Galilee. The first part of this section, 8:1–9:34, is a unit of narrative that tells of the activities of Jesus, including several miracle stories. Then 9:35–11:1 changes the focus. This portion of the larger section opens with a notice of Jesus' compassion and quickly records Jesus' message to the twelve prior to sending them to "the lost sheep of the house of Israel."

Structure. We can distinguish three large sub-sections in the full text for this Sunday. Matthew 9:35-38 reports Jesus' compassion for the crowds as he went about doing ministry. Then 10:1-4 tells of Jesus' authorizing the twelve, and it records their names. Finally 10:5-23 forms a collection of Jesus' instructions to the disciples as he sent them out in ministry. Any one of these sections could serve as a text for preaching. Indeed, there are a dozen or more potential texts in the materials in 10:5-23. Some focusing may prove necessary, because otherwise one confronts the difficulty of expressing a kaleidoscope of ideas in the limited time set aside for preaching.

Significance. In the broadest sense, this lesson is about compassion, commission, and conditions for mission. A sermon that would be more topical than expository (though related to the "sense" of the text) could work with these themes.

Matthew 9:35 essentially repeats Matthew 4:23, so that we gain no new information from this report of Jesus' activity. However, in the observations in vv. 36-38, we learn about the character of the ministry. First, the ministry was motivated by compassion. The crowds were genuinely needy, and Jesus cared for them. Second, Jesus had a sense of eschatological urgency in doing his work, and he communicates the pressure of the moment to his disciples. The time for extending the grace of God in work and deed to those in need is now, not "one of these days."

The authority that the disciples had for their work was given to them by Jesus. This authorization was not, however, like being tagged in a game of chase. It was not that once Jesus was "It" and now the disciples are. The Twelve were not left to run frantically by themselves. We cannot read this commissioning story in isolation from the Gospel in which it occurs. A glance at the ending of the

Gospel, which gives us the final commissioning story (last week's lesson), tells us that authority, in fact, resides with Christ. The risen Jesus empowers disciples for ministry and remains with them as the source of their direction and strength. In this manner, the disciples become Christ to others, and that is what it means to be faithful followers.

The collection of instructions in vv. 5-23 preserves a combination of time-bound traditions and "timeless truth," having mixed value for proclamation. For example, the historically specific recollection of the originally limited scope of Christ's mission in vv. 5-6 is more a matter for Bible study and the reconstruction of early Christian history than for preaching; but the pointed instructions in vv. 9-10 continue to remind us both that ministers are worthy of their pay and that, ultimately, the one who calls and commissions makes provisions for those who faithfully execute their callings. Similarly, the passage, which is cast as prophecy in vv. 16-20, contains information about the difficult conditions in which the earliest disciples labored, and it gives a strong word of encouragement for disciples who are facing difficulties in any era. These lines promise both stubborn human resistance and sufficient divine support for Christ's ministers.

For preaching, it may be necessary to focus deliberately on some sections of the text and to ignore judiciously other material. In turn, it may be helpful to create an abstract statement of the contents of the passage(s) which, without historical particularity, will govern the content and shape of the sermon.

Proper 6: The Celebration

Today's Gospel raises for us the interesting question of ministry and identity. The other Gospels list the apostles at the time of their calling (Mark 3; Luke 6), but Matthew makes the list at the point of their commissioning to proclaim the coming kingdom. They are identified with the work that Jesus gives them to do, rather than with some privileged relationship that they have with him on a private, personal basis. This identification can help make some sense of the old custom of naming a child formally at baptism, because baptism marks the beginning of a Christian's ministry. It is easier to understand why the pope takes a new name at his election, for that name will forever be identified with the form and content of his papal ministry, for better or worse. The expanded form of the Old Testament lesson has to do with naming and its significance. Isaac means "laughter," and so he will be always a reminder to his mother of her laughing disbelief and God's faithfulness. What kind of ministry do our names express individually? What kind of ministry does our church's name express in our community?

God's faithfulness, which is testified to in the Genesis lesson, is seen to be constant in Matthew, as the apostles are sent to "the lost sheep of the house of the Israel" and not to the Gentiles or the Samaritans. Preachers may need to help congregations understand this seeming exclusivity by distinguishing between the initial ministry to Israel prior to the Resurrection and the new ministry to all the world made possible by the Paschal victory. The agenda for ministry in today's Gospel has therefore become the Church's agenda in the world.

The epistle speaks of the length to which God's faithfulness will go: the God who gives a son to Sarah gives his own Son so that the world's weeping may be turned into laughter. This is the faithfulness of love, which is true passion that is willing to suffer and die for the beloved. This is not a sentimental, romantic love mistakenly thought to be everyone's right from God, a condition of the created order; it is a costly love that goes forth to give in the face of rejection, a love unmerited, undeserved by the beloved. And being so loved by such a faithful God, dying with Christ in baptism, we rise from the waters with laughter on our lips as we go to carry that message to the world.

Proper Seven Sunday Between June 19 and 25 Inclusive (If After Trinity Sunday)

Old Testament Texts

The Old Testament lesson of Hagar's salvation in the wilderness follows immediately upon the story of Sarah's miraculous birth that was the lesson for last week. Thus Genesis 21:8-21 provides a second story of salvation, but the context for understanding salvation shifts somewhat from last week. Instead of a miracle story to underscore how anything is possible for God—as was the case with Sarah—salvation this week is Hagar's liberation from oppression. An examination first of the setting of Hagar's story—as a sequel to Sarah's story of salvation—and then of its internal structure will provide the context for seeing the significance of this story—especially its two-sided character as being a story both of oppression and salvation. Psalm 86, minus the anger toward enemies, provides commentary on the two-sided message of this story.

The Lesson: *Genesis 21:8-21*

Liberation in Spite of God's People

Setting. As noted above, the story of Hagar is inseparable from the story of Sarah's miraculous birth. The conclusion of the latter story in Genesis 21:7—where Sarah poses the rhetorical question to us while breast feeding Isaac "Who would have thought that God could produce such a miraculous birth?"—is carried over into the new story in Genesis 21:8 with the notice that she has now weaned the child. The notice in v. 8 underscores that Sarah has lived with God's miracle of birth for some time, while her initial speech in v. 9 underscores how with the passing of time her exclusive focus on God and language of praise has now drifted to other matters such as the preservation of her child against Hagar and Ishmael.

Structure. The two structures below emphasize slightly different aspects in this story.

The first outline focuses on Hagar and Ishmael's salvation in the wilderness. When we read the story with an eye on Hagar and Ishmael, then its structure practically mirrors the story of Sarah's miraculous birth from last week, by dividing into two parts with an introduction (vv. 8-13) and a main section (vv. 14-21), and by alternating between narrative that provides a setting for speeches, and the actual discourse by different characters.

- I. Introduction (vv. 8-13)
  - A. Sarah's command to drive Hagar into the wilderness (vv. 8-10)
    - 1. Setting (vv. 8-9)
    - 2. Speech (v. 10)
  - B. The divine promise of progeny for Hagar (vv. 11-13)
    - 1. Setting (v. 11)
    - 2. Speech (vv. 12-13)
- II. The Salvation of Hagar and Ishmael in the Wilderness
  - A. The driving out of Hagar into the wilderness (vv. 14-16)
    - 1. Setting (vv. 14-15)
    - 2. Speech (v. 16*a*)
  - B. The salvation of Hagar in the wilderness (vv. 16*b*-21)
    - 1. Setting (vv. 16*b*)
    - 2. Speech (vv. 17-18)
    - 3. Divine action (vv. 19-21)

The second structure of the story highlights Sarah's oppressive role in the narrative and contrasts it with God's liberating activity. The outline provided above can also be used to illustrate this dimension of the story. Note how the introduction consists of two speeches that are in tension—Sarah's command to oppress Hagar for the sake of her son in v. 10 and the divine promise of progeny for Hagar in vv. 12-13. The second part of the story moves from speeches to actions in order to contrast the oppression of Sarah in vv. 14-16*a* and the salvation of God in vv. 16*b*-21.

Significance. The two structures suggest that the story of Hagar has different meanings to different readers. It is a story of how the people of God can utterly fail to internalize God's gift of salvation and, in so doing, actually become God's opponents. It is also a story of how God is able to liberate in spite of God's failed community. Each of these aspects of the story are important for preaching.

First, the story of Sarah. Sarah symbolizes the established people of God in this narrative. The previous story (in Genesis 18:1-15; 21:1-7) of her unbelief, her child's miraculous birth, and her final words of praise firmly fix her character. She is one who has been transformed through an experience of the salvation of God, and, while she holds the gift of salvation in her hands and breast-feeds Isaac, she has only words of praise for God. The juxtaposition of this portrait of Sarah in 21:1-7 with her wish in 21:10 to drive out Hagar and Ishmael underscores how quickly gifts of salvation can be reframed into the language of legal rights and how this changed attitude not only goes against the very nature of what salvation means, but can actually turn us into God's opponents. The motif of "laughter" (the name for Isaac) illustrates this sudden transformation in Sarah from being the recipient of God's salvation to becoming God's opponent.

In the commentary of last week the story of Sarah's miraculous birth ended with a pun on the motif of laughter in v. 6, when she used it as a joke on herself in order to praise God for the gift of Isaac. The motif of laughter reappears in v. 9, where it is no longer the language of divine praise, but now signifies Sarah's perceived threat to the rights of her son: "But Sarah saw the son of Hagar the Egyptian, whom she had borne to Abraham, playing." The word "playing" in this verse is the verbal form of the name Isaac in Hebrew, and it raises questions about what in fact may be the full range of meaning in the name *Isaac*. However we translate the activity of Ishmael—as playing or as laughing—the point of the story is that this child represents a threat to what Sarah perceives as her son's rights. And because of this perception she becomes the opponent of Hagar and even God.

Second, the story of Hagar and Ishmael. When the Old Testament lesson for this Sunday is read with Hagar in focus, it is a story of salvation, defined not so much as a miracle but as liberation from oppression. From this perspective it is an ironic story, because the oppressor is Sarah, and the one needing the liberating power of God is an Egyptian. That an Egyptian woman is a slave to an Israelite ancestor and then driven into the wilderness with little hope for survival is a story that is more familiar in the Book of Exodus where the roles are reversed. This ironic twist in the role of the characters underscores how the titles oppressor and oppressed are functional and not inherent to certain types or classes of people, which illustrates at least two things about salvation: first, that all are in need of it; and, second, that God's liberating power is open to all (even when the people of God would disagree).

The Response: *Psalm 86:1-10, 16-17*

An Individual Lament

Setting. Psalm 86 is a lament in which the psalmist requests help from God in a threatening situation and then lists a series of reasons why God should respond.

Structure. Scholars separate the lament in a number of different ways. The simplest is to divide the psalm beween vv. 1-13 and 14-17. In which case, the lament is interpreted as proceeding in two phases, with v. 14 signaling a new beginning or an intensification of the call for help. A more nuanced view of the language in the psalm yields smaller divisions, with vv. 1-7 being designated as a call for help, vv. 8-11 as a reflection on the character of God, vv. 12-13 as a vow to praise God, and vv. 14-17 as a renewed lament. The boundaries of the lectionary conforms to neither of these divisions but instead creates a new psalm that includes the initial lament and call for help in vv. 1-7, some reflection on the character of God in vv. 8-10, and a concluding call for help in vv. 16-17.

Significance. The psalm provides an important response to the Old Testament lesson by supplying language to Hagar's call for help in the wilderness. If the full psalm is used, then it is noteworthy that the insolent ones who are persecuting the psalmist in v. 14 must be read as the people of God themselves in this context.

New Testament Texts

The lesson from Romans 6 meditates upon the depths of the meaning of Christian life. The passage from Matthew 10 takes up the theme of disciples being witnesses for Christ and gives emphatic assurance that their final fate is in God's hands.

The Epistle: Romans 6:1*b*-11

Dead and Buried with Christ and Freed from Sin

Setting. Chapters 5–8 in Romans form a large unit concerned with the life of the Christian community as it experiences grace. Within these four chapters of Romans there are sub-units. Romans 6:1–7:6 forms one section of the larger whole, explaining how those who are justified live different than the manner in which they lived prior to God's gracious right-wising of them. Furthermore, within 6:1–7:6 there are three clear phases of Paul's argument. Our text, 6:1*b*-11, occurs within the first movement of Paul's reasoning, which comprises 6:1-14, a statement about Christians' transformation from death to life.

Structure. Paul forms his argument from an assumption that those reading the letter are themselves baptized. The chronology of Jesus' experience—death, burial, Resurrection—sets the markers for Paul's teaching about what it means for Christians to be "in Christ." There is constant motion back and forth between focusing on the Christians and focusing on Christ: we/Christ/we/Christ/we/Christ. Ultimately, in verse 11, Paul turns directly to the Romans, but even here he recognizes a thorough identification between the Romans and Christ, "So you must also consider yourselves dead to sin and alive to God in Christ."

Significance. This passage informs us, directly and indirectly, of several things. Indirectly, we can read between the lines to see that early Christians thought and taught about baptism in relation to Jesus' death (and perhaps burial); and they understood that through the death of Jesus some kind of gain was achieved and that somehow the benefits of Christ's death were transferred to the believers—either actually or symbolically in baptism. Paul assumes such thinking in mounting his argument to the Romans. He also assumes that the Romans will comprehend his statements, which build off the idea that Jesus Christ is a representative figure. Earlier (5:12-21) Paul treated Adam and Christ as universal representatives of humanity, speaking in apocalyptic categories about the "first" and "last Adam." Similarly, in Romans 3:21-25 Paul cast Christ Jesus as a universal human, taking up the language of the Jewish sacrificial cult to say that Christ died "for all who believe." In that same vein, here Paul applies the death, burial, and Resurrection of Christ to the lives of the Roman Christians. Paul explains what it means to be "in Christ" by stating how what happened to Christ has also happened to believers.

The lesson opens with a rhetorical question, advances with a strong declarative answer, and concludes by posing a further question—this time not so rhetorical as terribly real. Paul's concern: What does it mean that Christians are recipients of the benefits of grace? What real difference does grace make for believers' lives? Can there be a more pertinent question in all of Christian reflection?

Paul contemplates the past, the present, and the future of the Romans "in Christ." In their pasts, they died with Christ to sin. Paul understands that sin is a cosmic power—he even personifies it in his argument in Romans to dramatize its role in opposition to God. Effectively, sin deceived humanity and took humankind captive. Under the sway of the power of sin, humans were in bondage. Only when they died could humans escape sin's grasp. Christ himself freed humanity from sin by dying as a universal figure, so that through his death a benefit was won and, in turn, imparted to all who are now (as Paul would put it, by grace through faith) "in him." Also in the past, the Romans were symbolically buried with Christ in their baptism; and in the future, they will inherit the benefit of Christ's Resurrection as they will themselves be raised from the dead. This has profound meaning for the present. Believers are now freed from sin, because they died with Christ to sin. And as they look to the future in hope of resurrection, they are freed from sin and free for living a new life, which itself is a prolepsis of the resurrection life to come.

The mind-set behind this argument and its basic logic will seem strange to we whose imaginations have been stunted by a post-enlightenment scientific worldview. This passage articulates the mentality of poetry, not prose. How can we communicate such a message today? At the bowels of Paul's statements are these theological themes: grace, hope, and freedom. When approaching this powerful but difficult text, we remember that Paul is not evangelizing the Romans. He is standing alongside them and (1) calling up their past and (2) reminding them of their future, in order (3) to speak to them about the quality of their lives in the present. Grace, hope, and freedom are respectively the themes of these times. In preaching we may need to develop a temporal scheme similar to Paul's and, then, talk of the times by using metaphors and images appropriate to the particular theological theme of each time.

The Gospel: *Matthew 10:24-39*

Secure Despite Hostility for Declaring Christ's Words

Setting. This passage occurs in the second major section of Matthew's presentation of the ministry of Jesus. It follows on the heels of the lesson for last Sunday, so for fuller information about the framing of this text in its literary context please consult the section on setting for last week's Gospel lesson. Jesus is depicted as addressing the twelve concerning the ministry to which he directs them, immediately prior to their being sent out by him. In general 10:24-42 deals with the nature and cost of discipleship.

Structure. The lesson falls into four distinct, but related, parts. First, vv. 24-25 speak of the relationship of disciple and master. Second, vv. 26-31 tell the disciples "whom to fear," and embedded in this pronouncement is a directive to proclaim the teaching of Christ (v. 27). Third, vv. 32-33 comment on the determinative importance of acknowledging or denying Christ before humanity. Fourth, vv. 34-39 speak of the paradoxical, controversial, and absolute character of Christ and his call to discipleship.

Significance. Although these sayings are cast as being delivered to the Twelve before their going out from Jesus to minister, the majority of the statements are relevant to the lives of all disciples. The opening verses (24-25) combine the metaphors of disciple/teacher and servant/master to fix the notion of discipleship to Christ in terms of service. A normal disciple/teacher relationship might sometimes produce a student who would be "above" or superior to the teacher; but Christian discipleship is not like that. Instead, Christ's disciples are called to be like their teacher/master, Christ. The very word *Christian* (not found in Matthew, but appearing first in Acts 11:26) means "little-Christ," and was almost certainly applied to the disciples as a term of derision. Remarkably, the name-calling stuck, and the moniker faithfully names Christ's disciples in terms that Jesus would approve ("It is enough for the disciple to be like the teacher"—v. 25).

The following remark about calling the master of the house "Beelzebul" is related to Matthew 12:24, where Jesus' opponents say "It is only by Beelzebul, the ruler of the demons, that this fellow casts out the demons." Matthew's sequence is noteworthy. He reported a similar remark in 9:34, but the name *Beelzebul* does not occur in that passage; so that this prediction by Jesus becomes a double-prediction, part of which will be fulfilled in the telling of the rest of the Gospel story. In turn, for later Christians who experienced persecution, these words from Jesus would reinforce the validity of their discipleship. Experiencing hostility is not an indication of failure in following (nor is it necessarily an indication of faithfulness—perhaps one is simply obnoxious), it may be the validation of our Christian service. And, indeed, if life is smooth and carefree, perhaps one should wonder whether one is living up to Christ's call.

The prediction of persecution is followed by teaching about fear and fearlessness in vv. 26-31. Three items in these lines demand attention. First, woven into the statements about fearing and not fearing is a direction to carry forward in an amplified form the teaching of Jesus. The words of comfort about God's care for disciples and the prescriptions on fearlessness are not simply general statements for all times and places. They are focused admonitions and promises in relation to the faithful proclamation of the message of Christ.

Disciples are called to speak for their master as a crucial part of discipleship.

Second, the capacity of the disciples to be fearlessly faithful is rooted in the faithfulness of God. The disciples are not merely told, "Be brave!" as if they were a group of Cub Scouts walking through the woods at night. Instead, they are reminded of the care of the Creator God for all creation, and they are declared to be an important part of the creation.

Third, the line about "whom to fear" contains a genuine ambiguity. What is clear is that the disciples are not to fear other humans, but what is not clear is the identity of the one they are to fear. Some interpreters suggest it is Satan, and others contend it is God. That the reference is to Satan seems more likely for two reasons: (a) the mention of Gehenna or Hell, and (b) the contrast with the following remarks about the deep concern of God for the disciples. Nevertheless, what is striking in the sequence of Jesus' sayings is that fear of final condemnation (by Satan or by God) is to motivate the disciples to completely trust God, who deeply cares for them.

Verses 32-33 are Matthew's version of a tradition that Luke preserves in a slightly different form. In Luke it is "the Son of Man" who will acknowledge or deny persons before "the angels of God" on the basis of their acknowledgment or denial of Jesus. Luke's version seems more primitive, and, if so, we can see that Matthew offers this statement from a post-Easter perspective. He and the Church have identified "the Son of Man" with the risen Jesus. This means that the issue of acknowledgment and denial is related to the full gospel message and not merely to recognizing or failing to recognize the historical Jesus. "Stand up, stand up for Jesus" means more than admitting he was a "great guy"; disciples are called to a full commitment to the lordship of the risen Christ.

Verses 34-39 are complex and difficult, but enticing. The dramatic images are surely hyperbolic, but through the course of Christian history, the words of this striking passage have often been literally true. The earliest followers of Jesus experienced genuine hardships as they lived as faithful disciples. Similarly, others like Francis of Assisi, Saint Catherine, and Martin Luther have had family relationships altered and even destroyed because they sought to be true to their Christian callings.

Jesus' words seem harsh. He demands an uncompromised devotion, yet notice that this difficult teaching ends with a bold promise: Those who give their lives to Christ without reservation, steadily refusing to live in compromise to this world's demands, are assured that the investment of life in discipleship to Christ imbues life itself with divinely intended meaning.

Proper 7: The Celebration

The Old Testament lesson and the Gospel deal with the subject of persecution. In the first case, we are told about persecution carried on by those blessed by God (Abraham and Sarah drive out Hagar and Ishmael); in the second case we are told that our faithfulness as disciples will result in persecution. It is significant to find that in both cases God appears to be on the side of the oppressed rather than the oppressor.

The preacher is faced with the issue of persecution as validation of faithfulness or citizenship in the kingdom. The Church has had to deal from the beginning with the "gung ho" who sought persecution and even martyrdom. Such an attitude is works righteousness carried to an extreme. Perhaps today's Gospel needs to be turned on its head as we define persecution in North America as not being persecuted, since we are doing an excellent job of accommodating the Gospel to our culture without the threat of fire and sword! A re-reading of Bonhoeffer's *The Cost of Discipleship* will be helpful homework in preparing to preach on this text. "Those who are still afraid of men have no fear of God, and those who have fear of God have ceased to be afraid of men. All preachers of the gospel will do well to recollect this saying daily" (p. 195).

The exhortation to confess Christ before the world is certainly pertinent in a society that is as embarrassed by verbal professions of faith, however mild (unless they are vapid professions of faith in faith), as eighteenth-century English society was by enthusiasm. And the problem is complicated by a general agreement that it is more important to practice what you preach than to preach it, since actions speak louder than words. The preacher might wish to raise a couple of objections to this subtle form of socially acceptable persecution that silences Christian witness.

Preaching what we practice is important because it keeps us connected to the theological reason for activity. Some of us perform actions of Christian witness, but we hesitate to point to the reason for our deed for fear of appearing to be the fanatic evangelist or the buttonholing manipulator. We end up with the credit, not Christ. It becomes our work, not God's. And we no longer have to make those distinctions between what we do on our own and what we know we can do only because Christ works within us. We speak much of the priesthood of all believers as though priests are not theologians, yet many laity have at age fifty not had a theological discussion since age fifteen. In physical maturity they are spiritual adolescents. If we fail to preach what we practice, we run the risk of forgetting Christ. The baptismal rite of the Episcopal Church expresses our obligation in no uncertain terms. At the conclusion of the service the minister and the congregation say to the newly baptized: "Confess the faith of Christ crucified, proclaim his resurrection, and share with us in his eternal priesthood" (*The Book of Common Prayer,* p. 308).

Proper Eight
Sunday Between June 26 and July 2 Inclusive

Old Testament Texts

The Old Testament texts for this Sunday are about divine testing. Genesis 22:1-14 is the story of how God tested Abraham in commanding the sacrifice of Isaac, while Psalm 13 is a lament that provides liturgical language for how we approach God during times of testing.

The Lesson: *Genesis 22:1-14*

To Fear God Is to See God

Setting. The story of Genesis 22 is sinister. God's command for Abraham to sacrifice Isaac in the opening verse is outrageous, and, even though the narrative progresses to a solution that bypasses the execution of the opening command, the reader cannot help leaving this story with a shudder. In Genesis 22 the divine request is too big and too terrifying to be resolved by the narrative logic of the story line. Or, to say it another way, the gap between the opening divine command and our own sense of ethics and of how God should act in this world are never really brought back together in the story. Consequently, even though a ram ends up burning on the altar instead of a boy, unsettling images linger about the God of Abraham. We leave this story somewhat relieved to be out of it in one piece and with the frightening realization that we do not really know very much about this God. From the story, we do know that there is a vast distance between who God is and our limited understanding of him, which means that the life of faith will be one of constant testing, because the believer will frequently be called to act without fully understanding.

In such situations, action taken out of a fear of God must suffice. The story of Abraham's journey to the mountain of God to fulfill an incomprehensible divine command is such a story where fear of God is in fact perception of God.

Structure. The local geography is central for interpreting Genesis 22:1-14, and it also determines how the story is structured. After vv. 1-2 introduce the central theme of testing at a specific mountain that God would show Abraham, the central section of the narrative in vv. 3-13 traces in three parts the journey of Abraham to the summit of the Mountain of the Lord where the test takes place, and then the story concludes in v. 14 with an aetiology of the place—an account of the naming of Moriah. The story can be outlined in the following manner.

I. Introduction: The Test (vv. 1-2)
   A. The description of Isaac as Abraham's only son
   B. The divine command to sacrifice
   C. The location of a mountain in Moriah
II. The Initial Three Day Journey to the Designated Place (vv. 3-5)
   A. The description of the journey
   B. Abraham's perception of the place: "Abraham lifted up his eyes and saw the place from afar."
   C. The sending away of the servants
III. The Journey of Abraham and Isaac to the Mountain (vv. 6-8)
   A. The description of the journey
   B. Isaac's question about the sacrifice
   C. Abraham's reply: "God will see it—the lamb to sacrifice, my son."
IV. The Sacrifice on the Mountain (vv. 9-13)
   A. The attempted sacrifice of Isaac
   B. The divine intervention and speech: "Now I know that you fear God."
   C. Abraham's perception of the ram: "And Abraham lifted his eyes and saw . . . a ram."
   D. The sacrifice of the ram
V. Conclusion (v. 14)
   Abraham's naming of the mountain: "God sees" and "On the Mountain of the Lord it will be seen."

Significance. Genesis 22 is a story of testing. Any interpretation of the story requires that two questions be answered: How is Abraham tested by God? and Where is he tested?

First, how is Abraham tested? The testing of Abraham concerns his perception of God. Thus the motif of "seeing" (especially of what Abraham sees or says that he sees) is central to the story. In order to interpret the importance of this motif, however, we must depart from the NRSV translation. The Hebrew word for "to see" occurs four times in the story in the following forms: (vv. 4, *wayyar'*; 8, *yir'eh*; 13, *wayyar'*; and 14, *yir'eh*). If we look more closely, it becomes clear that the four occurrences are really a two-part repetition: vv. 4 and 13 repeat the phrase, "And Abraham lifted up his eyes and saw (*wayyar'*) . . . the place/a ram," while vv. 8, 14 repeat the phrase, "God/the Lord sees or will see (*yir'eh*)." Note that the NRSV has translated vv. 8 and 14 as "God/the Lord provides or will provide," which obscures the important role of the motif of "seeing" in carrying the meaning of the story. Check the footnote in your Bible and you will see that in fact the word that is translated "provide" is in Hebrew the word for "see."

The two-part repetition of vv. 4, 8 and vv. 13, 14 illustrates the testing of Abraham in the following manner. Verses 4, 8 occur during Abraham's journey to the mountain of God. The notice in v. 4 that "Abraham lifted his eyes and saw the place" is ominous in the development of the story because it signals the impending child sacrifice. Abraham's reply in v. 8 to the question of Isaac about the content of the sacrifice heightens the tension even further, for his statement is ambiguous. A literal translation of the Hebrew would be, "God will see it—the lamb to sacrifice, my son." The object of what God will see (the "it") is not clear. The statement could be a confession that God would provide a substitute for Isaac (as the NRSV translation suggests) in which case the "it" is the lamb and both are distinct from the "son," but the "it" and the "lamb" and the "son" could also be identified as the same referents, in which case Abraham is simply stating the opening divine command that the son will be the lamb for this sacrifice and that God will see it. The repetition in vv. 13 and 14 has none of the ominous quality of vv. 4, 8, because these verses occur after God stops the sacrifice of Isaac in vv. 11-12. Now when Abraham "lifts up his eyes and sees" it is not the impending location of a child sacrifice, but a substitute for the boy in the form of a ram. Furthermore, when Abraham repeats the statement that "God sees," it is no longer ambiguous but clearly a confession of salvation.

The key to the story that has allowed for the transformation from ambiguity to confession between the two parts is the divine speech in vv. 11-12. Just when Abraham was ready to kill his son, God intervenes with the words, "Now I know that you fear God." The Hebrew word meaning "to fear" in this statement is a pun with the word meaning "to see," for it is spelled almost the same, *yere'*. The central point of the story for preaching is that Abraham was willing to act solely out of his fear of God, even when he could not see clearly the logic of the divine command. In doing this, he passed the test, and also reached a new insight about God, namely that God is present ("God sees") even in situations where we do not clearly see God.

Second, where is Abraham tested? The test of Abraham did not take place just anywhere. It took place specifically on the Mountain of God, which in this story is named Moriah (which may translate from the Hebrew "The Lord sees."). The imagery of divine mountains in the Old Testament symbolizes different worship settings (see Year A, First Sunday of Advent). With this information as background, we recognize that the testing of Abraham at Mount Moriah is a story about worship, which raises the question of whether God is present in worship, even when we may not perceive it or when the events around us go against our own sense of ethics and against our understanding of how God should act in this world. When preaching the story from this perspective it is clear that in worship we must act out of our fear of God, even when we do not see God clearly, because even at these times we can be confident that God does see us. This understanding of God makes it possible for the people of God to lament with the words of Psalm 13.

The Response: *Psalm 13*

Addressing God in Darkness

Setting. Psalm 13 is a lament. Lamentations frequently take place in worship when the psalmist feels that God is very distant or absent from worship altogether. Such moments are situations of blindness that test our faith in God's reliability. Psalm 13 is such a lament that provides liturgical language on how we approach God during times of testing.

Structure. Psalm 13 separates into three parts. Verses 1-2 consist of a series of desperate questions by the psalmist: How long Lord? Verses 3-4 build off the opening questions by asking God to break the silence and to allow the psalmist to see again the presence of God. Verses 5-6 shift to the language of confidence and faith that the psalmist will one day see God again.

Significance. Psalm 13 provides commentary on the testing of Abraham in Genesis 22, for it also addresses the problem of blindness that results from God far exceeding our understanding. The psalm does not provide the situation of the psalmist, all we know is that the psalmist is not able to see God. In view of this situation, the language moves through three parts: from complaint in vv. 1-2, to request in vv. 3-4, and finally to confidence in vv. 5-6. The central request in the middle section is that the psalmist be allowed to see God once again ("lighten my eyes"). The confidence in vv. 5-6 is not because the request is answered. Rather it is a statement about the future based on past trust. Notice how the language moves from past to future: I trusted (past), and my heart will rejoice (future); I will sing (future), because he has dealt bountifully with me (past). The language of lament is possible because we have a history with God that is bigger than the present moment. Thus we can know that God is present (that God sees) even in situations when we do not clearly see God.

New Testament Texts

The epistle from Romans 6 ponders the meaning of Christian freedom. The Gospel from Matthew 10 advances the focus of the past two weeks by moving to the image of receiving Christ and his followers to declare the value of righteousness, which in Matthew is living according to God's standards.

The Epistle: *Romans 6:12-23*

Freed from Sin and Freed for Righteousness

Setting. We have regularly observed that Romans 5–8 is a major section of the letter, which contemplates the meaning of Christian life as the experience of grace. Within these four chapters, there are recognizable units and subunits of thought. Commentators almost universally treat 6:1-14 as a piece contemplating the meaning of grace in terms of "freedom from sin" and 6:15-23 as a complementary section stressing the significance of grace as "freedom for righteousness." The lesson dips into both these units and gives us snippets of each interpretation of the life of grace.

Structure. Verse 12 is an odd place to begin the reading for the line opens, "Therefore, . . . " clearly referring to the foregoing argument in order to draw conclusions from it and beyond it. Nevertheless, the admonitions and conclusions Paul begins to advance in v. 12 continue through vv. 13-14. Then in v. 15, Paul poses a rhetorical question that sets up the next section of his reflection: "What then? Should we sin because we are not under law but under grace?" He launches his argument in v. 15*b* and continues to develop his position through v. 23, though his mood is more explanatory than hortatory in vv. 19-22.

Significance. Paul's point in 6:1-11 (the argument upon which vv. 12-14 build) is summarized neatly in v. 11, "So you also must consider yourselves dead to sin and alive to God in Christ Jesus." In other words, the Romans had once been spiritually dead because they had been in the grasp of the power of sin. In that state, they were cut off from living obediently in relation to God. But now they are alive in Christ because his death incorporated them into God's grace, which defeated the power of sin.

With this starting point established, Paul continues, "Therefore, . . ." Through Christ Jesus, God did for the Romans what they could not do for themselves: God set them free from the power of sin. Now Paul reminds the Romans that they have real responsibilities in relation to the freedom that has been given them in Christ. Since they are freed from sin, they must reject the bidding of sin as it makes its appeal to them through the still sin-stained structures of human life. The Romans have a choice to make, and it is one they could not have made before the coming of Christ. Paul calls them to choose God and God's ways. In sin's grasp, the Romans had no choice, but the freedom of grace allows them to select whom they will obey and what they will do. Paul's point is that grace brings real freedom and freedom requires responsibility. Strikingly, Paul does not assume that humans are free, rather they are in bondage to sin; but the power of grace sets sin's slaves (humans) free and endows them with the responsibility to choose their master. In Romans the gospel of grace means, first, that humans have been set free from their former bondage to sin and, second, that they are called to exercise the responsibility for living obediently in relationship to God in the power of God's grace.

Lest the Romans misunderstand him, Paul gives his point a new twist in v. 15: One can elect, in the freedom of grace, to serve the power of sin, but that certainly does not mean that one should do so. Indeed, exactly the opposite is the case—the Romans "should" become slaves to righteousness. All this advice is excellent, but Paul seems to know that it may transcend comprehension; so he brings matters down to a very practical level in v. 19. Lives lived toward God look different than lives lived in bondage to sin. Paul speaks in terms the Romans would have understood, showing disapproval of "impurity" and "iniquity." This language is ancient religious "boundary terminology," referring to that which complies with the standards of a definable religious persuasion. Put theologically, Paul is talking about doing and not doing God's will, usually as it has been understood through revelation. The locus or norm of God's revelation is named in v. 23: Christ Jesus our Lord. The freedom that Christians receive by God's grace can be abused, but that is not the purpose for which God granted the freedom. Rather, God freed us so that we can and will live in conformity to the person and the work of Jesus Christ. He is to be our Lord, and it is he whom we are to serve. The real goal and meaning of freedom is in such a life of service.

The Gospel: *Matthew 10:40-42*

The Costs and Rewards of Discipleship

Setting. These verses bring to a conclusion the section of the Gospel that began in 9:35 and with which we have been concerned during the past two weeks. Jesus has spoken with the Twelve about the way they are to go about ministry, the conditions they will face, the costs of faithful service, and the divine security that will be theirs amidst difficulties. Here Jesus continues to speak about the price of discipleship and the rewards of service. The verse which follows the reading for today, 11:1, brings the second section of Matthew's presentation of Jesus' ministry to a conclusion.

Structure. Prior to vv. 40-42 is a cluster of several sayings. Verses 34-39 focus on the controversy and conflict that Jesus' ministry brings and their effects on the lives of his disciples. Notice there are three distinct and difficult sayings: conflict in the family (vv. 34-36—v. 35 quotes, without citing overtly, Micah 7:6); Christ before family and self (vv. 37-39); and finding and losing one's life (v. 39). Then vv. 40-42 assemble three somewhat similar sayings in a deliberate order that advances a linear argument about rewards for faithful service: receiving disciples as Christ and, in turn, God (v. 40); receiving a prophet or a righteous person (v. 41); and giving refreshment to an ordinary disciple (v. 42).

Significance. The first group of sayings are often referred to as Jesus' "hard words," because (1) they predict and promise difficulties in family life and (2) they call for a radical devotion to Christ. The "sword" Jesus says he came to bring is the divisiveness that will result in social structures, even or especially family life, because of disciples' loyalty to their master. The "normal" Jewish expectation for the coming of the Messiah was that he would bring peace. These sayings do not mean that Jesus was malevolent, but that there would be those who would reject him, his message, and in turn his disciples. Such division cuts deeply into the most personal relationships, but, nevertheless, Jesus does not change his line or accommodate those who would seek to avoid the conflict. Instead, he states plainly the necessity of placing him above all else. To what are we called with these words? To full devotion to our risen Lord and to the standards which he set forth in the course of his ministry—namely, to selfless service, to compassion at all costs, to a faith in God that orients our lives toward others rather than toward ourselves. But why should such standards create controversy? In fact, history provides us with concrete answers. Religions tend to focus on the rigidity of rules and the security of regulations rather than toward the risky business of active discipleship. Humans tend to domesticate the powerful stuff of primary religious experience. We want rules, so we can know exactly what to do and not to do to make sure we will get our just rewards. Bluntly, what benefits we get. The prospect of service that pays no big dividends is not overly attractive. A survey sought to determine why people attended church. The answers: It's good for the children. It helps you work harder. It makes you feel better. It improves the community. No one in the survey mentioned service.

Yet, as the Gospel reveals in vv. 40-42, there are those who answer Christ's calling and who do live lives of discipleship. To these Christ speaks of rewards. Above all, there is the reward of a relationship with other disciples, Christ, and God. This provides the joy of community, and it probably provides much more. Christ himself came in service, and as we receive others in his name, we receive him. In his company, we will be led to new avenues of service. There is a remarkable circularity in this pattern of relationship that locks us in and strengthens us for doing the tough work of Jesus Christ in a broken, bleeding, and dying world. In service to Christ and in the presence of Christ, we experience the depths of the joy of service. Thus we find and lose ourselves to discover ourselves found and rewarded by Christ.

Proper 8: The Celebration

Today's epistle is also appointed each year for the Easter Vigil when the Church receives new members through Holy Baptism. It serves then as a reminder of our baptism and may provide the scriptural warrant for the administration of baptism on this Sunday. Too frequently baptisms are administered "on demand" with no relationship to the liturgical day or season or the lessons appointed for the day. The result is a privatization of the sacrament and a loss of its ecclesiological base. The pastor and worship committee should consult each other to plan baptismal occasions for the year, so that they are a part of the church's corporate life rather than a quick intrusion into the service. For most parishes four times a year should be sufficient for baptisms (if quarterly communion, why not quarterly baptism?). Easter is the primary occasion (dying and being raised with Christ), followed by Pentecost at the end of Eastertide (reminding us that all baptism is Spirit-baptism). The Baptism of the Lord, the first

Sunday after Epiphany, is another occasion (reminding us that baptism is inauguration into ministry), and All Saints' Day or the Sunday following (reminding us that baptism is the making of a saint, one set apart for service). If more occasions for baptism are required, they should be chosen in relation to one or more of the lessons, so that the sacrament is seen as a form of proclamation within the assembly of the people of God. This advance designation of baptismal Sundays serves to emphasize that baptism is a corporate and not an individualistic occasion—usually more than one baptism will be administered. This planned approach also allows for the scheduling of preparation classes for catechumens or parents and sponsors, thus keeping baptism and instruction in the faith united.

If there are no baptisms on this day, the epistle still provides the opportunity to preach about the sacrament and its place and meaning in Christian experience. Martin Luther uses baptism as a sign of God's faithfulness when he discusses the tempting of Abraham, today's Old Testament lesson. Luther points out that the command to sacrifice Isaac flew in the face of the earlier promise that from him should come a great nation, but that Abraham was obedient to the command because he trusted God to keep the promise, in spite of all appearances to the contrary. Luther continues:

> Therefore one should hold fast to this comfort, that what God has once declared, this He does not change. You were baptized, and in Baptism the kingdom of God was promised you. You should know that this is His unchangeable Word, and you should not permit yourself to be drawn away from it. [*Works*, vol. 4, p. 96]

The Gospel's saying today about the primacy of our love for God may also be used with Abraham as an illustration of what that means. Baptism is again illustrative, in that it is the way we lose our lives in order to gain life.

Proper Nine Sunday Between July 3 and 9 Inclusive

Old Testament Texts

Genesis 24 is the story of how the servant of Abraham searches for a wife for Isaac in Mesopotamia and finds Rebekah. Psalm 45:10-17 is the second half of a Marriage Song that focuses on the bride.

The Lesson: *Genesis 24:34-38, 42-49, 58-67*

A Story with Many Heroes

Setting. In many ways the testing of Abraham in Genesis 22 (the lectionary lesson for last week) concludes the Abrahamic cycle of stories in Genesis even though his death is not recorded until Genesis 25. The story of Abraham began in Genesis 12:1-4*a* by underscoring his faith in leaving his native country to follow the call of God and by outlining the divine promise of progeny that would be his reward for faithfulness. The divine command to sacrifice Isaac in Genesis 22 completes the story of Abraham, because it was the ultimate test of his faith, and, as we saw last week, it ended with a renewal of the divine promise of progeny that began his story in Genesis 12:1-4*a*. Genesis 23:1–25:18 is an anticlimactic section of the book of Genesis. It has none of the drama and suspense of Genesis 22. Instead, this section of literature cleans up loose ends that are left over from the story of Abraham and Sarah. Genesis 23 narrates the death and burial of Sarah, while Genesis 25 provides further genealogical information about Abraham and Ishmael, as well as noting the death of Abraham.

Genesis 24 is sandwiched between these obituaries, and the loose end to which it is addressed is a wife for Isaac. A wife for Isaac, of course, is far more than a loose end, for it goes to the heart of the ancestral stories: without a wife there can be no progeny, and without progeny God's promise to Abraham fails.

Yet this important event—a wife for Isaac—is framed between two obituaries and told in such a matter-of-fact way that we must remind ourselves just how important this narrative is to the larger story of Genesis. The strong message in preaching Genesis 24 may very well be the lack of drama that takes place in the telling of the story of Rebekah and how she married Isaac.

Structure. Genesis 24 is an extended chapter, which separates into four parts: vv. 1-9 are an account of Abraham instructing his servant to go back to Mesopotamia to find a wife for Isaac; vv. 10-27 narrate the servant's encounter with Rebekah at the well outside of the city of Nahor; vv. 28-61 are an extended section in which the servant recounts the entire story to the kinsmen of Rebekah, Laban and Bethuel; and vv. 62-67 describe the return journey and the marriage of Isaac and Rebekah. The lectionary text includes verses from only the third and fourth parts.

- I. The Command of Abraham Concerning a Wife for Isaac (vv. 1-4)
- II. The Servant and Rebekah at the Well (vv. 10-21)
  - A. The time and location: evening at the well (vv. 10-11)
  - B. The servants prayer for a sign (vv. 12-14)
  - C. The actions of Rebekah (vv. 15-20)
  - D. The servants meditation (v. 21)
- III. Rebekah's Agreement to Marry Isaac (vv. 28-61)
- IV. The Marriage (vv. 62-67)
  - A. The time and location: evening in the Negeb (vv. 62-63)
  - B. Rebekah's perception of Isaac (vv. 64-65)
  - C. The servant's recounting of the story (v. 66)
  - D. Isaac marries Rebekah (v. 67)

Significance. The outline illustrates the central problem that must be addressed in interpreting this story—namely, determining who is the central character. Who is the hero of the story? Is it Abraham because he initiates the story with an act of faith? Is it the servant who provides most of the action and demonstrates faith through his prayer at the well? Is it Rebekah who shows hospitality to the servant and who agrees to leave her family in much the same way that Abraham once did? Is it Laban and Bethuel who agree to send Rebekah into an unknown future because they perceive the hand of God in these events? Is it Isaac who marries Rebekah? Then, finally, what are we to make with the closing reference to Sarah? Is this story to fill a gap that her death has brought about? Genesis 24 evokes dull drama because so many characters participate in the narrative. Thus we do not know whose story it is, and it becomes difficult for the reader to focus on any one person. Then, too, the banality is further highlighted because this narrative is sandwiched between two obituaries, where it appears to function as a denouement after the breathtaking story of Genesis 22.

The problem of Genesis 24 is the key to its interpretation, but it requires reframing. The task of interpretation in Genesis 24 is not to determine who is the primary hero of the story, but to recognize that all the characters have a heroic role in this narrative. This is a story of how God works out divine promises through the interrelationship of many people doing good but not exceptional things. This is not a story about a father who is willing to sacrifice his only son for God. Rather, it is a story about a father who is trying to discern the will of God with regard to his son's marriage. It is a story about a servant, a woman, and an extended family all of whom try to do the right thing in the everyday routine of their lives. And, as each of these characters tries to discern the will of God at some juncture in the story, eventually a narrative emerges that is no less significant than Genesis 22, for the promise of God would end if Isaac weren't married, just as it would have if he were sacrificed by Abraham. The central message for preaching Genesis 24 is that it is a story about many characters whose collective participation brings about a heroic act—namely, the carrying on of God's promise to a new generation. When preparing to preach this text, you may want to reflect on how your congregation mirrors Genesis 24.

The Response: *Psalm 45:10-17*

A Marriage Song

Setting. Psalm 45 is a Song of Marriage. Scholars speculate on its original function, whether it may have been a liturgy for all marriages in the later period of ancient Israel or a celebration of the king's marriage. The latter interpretation seems more probable, which has prompted the classification of the song as a Royal Psalm.

Structure. The lectionary reading is limited to the latter half of the psalm. It is helpful, however, to see the larger structure of the psalm, which separates into four parts.

I. Introduction (v. 1)
II. Praise of the King (Bridegroom) (vv. 2-9)
III. Praise of the Queen (Bride) (vv. 10-15)
IV. Conclusion (vv. 16-17)

Significance. Two uses of this psalm are possible. First, it could be used in the worship service as a celebration of marriage, in which case the entire psalm would be more appropriate. If the entire psalm is read, it would provide commentary on the outcome of the story in Genesis 24. Second, the psalm could be limited to the second half, in which case it becomes a celebration of Rebekah and her ability to leave Nahor to follow God's call to marry Isaac. Either reading is appropriate in connection to Genesis 24.

New Testament Texts

The readings continue the sequence undertaken during the weeks of ordinary time following Pentecost. The text from Romans is Paul's well-known speech, "Wretched man that I am!" In Matthew Jesus speaks bluntly to his audience, uttering woes and calling the weary to him.

The Epistle: *Romans 7:15-25*a

Delivered from the Body of Death

Setting. Commentators almost universally view Romans 7:7-25 as a concerted discussion within the larger section of the letter, Romans

5–8. The initial six verses (7-12) clarify the nature of the law and point to the real problem that humans confront—namely sin which uses even the "holy and just and good" commandments to lead humans into a deception unto death. Verse 13 summarizes the argument set forth in vv. 7-12. Then v. 14 introduces a new direction in the reflection (discernible by the shift in Greek to the present tense) by picking up the logic of the foregoing verses and labeling the law and humanity "spiritual" and "of the flesh, sold into slavery under sin" respectively. It is unfortunate that the lesson begins with v. 15 rather than with v. 7, or at least v. 13, for without the previous discussion (or at least the summary in v. 13) one can easily, and mistakenly, come to Paul's "I" language in vv. 15-25 and assume that the apostle is giving us a bit of serious personal introspection. Nothing could be farther from the mark. The "I" of our lesson is a representative figure of all humankind, the typical "fleshly sinner" who speaks not merely for Paul but for the universal human experience in bondage to sin and death.

Structure. In the lesson, vv. 15-20 take up the universal experience of humanity in being grasped by sin and rendered incapable of doing even what one knows is right. The experience is one of utter frustration, and as humanity is caught in this dilemma there is no perception of hope, rather there is a universal hopelessness. Then, vv. 21-25 express, first, the sense of despair that humankind experiences as sin dominates, despite the best intentions and, second, the hope of humanity in the work of God through Jesus Christ. Encountering the hope allows the Christian to assess life frankly, and v. 25 completes this reflection with such a candid appraisal.

Significance. No part of Romans is more difficult, profound, or subject to misinterpretation than the section from which this lesson is drawn. In our current psychologically oriented era, we are almost certain to see Paul speaking personally and confessionally in this text. Read, however, in the context of Paul's letters in general and the flow of the argument in Romans in particular, and read in the light of ancient thought and rhetoric, we see that Paul is speaking as the "universal human." The voice in this passage is far more nearly that of Adam than that of Paul.

In a nutshell, Paul says that without Jesus Christ humanity is up the swift-flowing creek of sin without a paddle—and with a bad leak in the boat. Paul shifts in these verses from discussing the relationship of sin and the law (a tragic and deceptive relationship for humanity) to contrasting "the good" and "sin." "The good" is equivalent to God's will, and while the law has something to do with this, Paul does not limit but broadens the focus in this passage to deal with God's will in an unrestricted sense.

Paul declares a shocking truth, namely that sin has the power to dupe humanity into the most hopeless situation. Sin can use genuine devotion to God, specifically strict concern with adherence to the law as an absolutely accurate statement of God's will for humanity, to produce exactly the reverse of our purposes. Duped by sin, humans have an inauthentic relationship to God in the place of the genuine intimacy that they sought and desired. This lesson recognizes the sinister nature of the power of sin and the tragic situation of humankind.

When using this text for preaching, one must work to take evil seriously and to register the plight of humanity under the influence of sin or evil. This will be no casual task. Our world easily and regularly plays down the power of sin. We reduce sin to the sum total of human misdeeds, a reduction that would appall the apostle. Paul understood that there were forces at work in this world that were both external to humans and diametrically opposed to God. Paul believed in evil far more than we do. Part of Paul's message is the frank recognition of the forces that deceive humans, even well-intentioned humans, into serving evil. Frighteningly, humans are most thoroughly deceived when they think they are serving God, but when, in fact, they are serving evil. This passage calls us to make this point in proclamation; and sadly, illustrations abound.

Only when we see our hopeless situation is the gospel heard as the good news that it is. What is the hope of a pitifully deceived humanity? Jesus Christ (read v. 25*a*). Paul says that Jesus Christ liberated us from the deception of sin. Paul does not say how, but we may infer the answer. Humans who were intent upon serving God crucified Jesus in order to rid themselves and God of a seemingly perverse nuisance. But God exposed the error of humanity's ways and the righteousness of Jesus as God's power raised Jesus from the grave—in both condemnation and vindication—exposing the error of sin-directed devotion and the hope of liberation in Jesus Christ.

The Gospel: *Matthew 11:16-19, 25-30*

Amidst Misunderstanding, Christ Calls to Comprehension and Action

Setting. The third major section of Matthew's five-part presentation of the ministry of Jesus begins at 11:2 and continues through 13:53. Although Matthew shows us that Jesus encountered resentment and disbelief in the earlier portions of his ministry, it is in this third section that the strong resistance to Jesus' work emerges in anticipation of the forthcoming rejection of Jesus in the Passion narrative (chapters 26–27). In chapters 11–12, Matthew reports a series of questions that were put to Jesus, his responses, controversies in which he engaged, and condemnations that he uttered.

In chapter 11, messengers come from John the Baptist asking Jesus, "Are you the one who is to come, or are we to wait for another?" Jesus answered in prophetic speech, and, then, he continued by speaking to the crowds about the Baptist (we examined this material during the Third Sunday of Advent in Year A). The lesson for this Sunday takes the speech about the Baptist as a point of departure. Now, Jesus speaks directly to "this generation" about their poor reception of both the Baptist and himself. In turn, Jesus utters woes, offers thanks to God for the work of divine revelation, and appeals to the "weary" to come to him. The subsequent section reports a series of controversies between Jesus and the Pharisees.

Structure. There are two main parts to the lesson. Verses 16-19 speak to "this generation" about the way it received the Baptist and "the Son of Man" (Jesus). Verses 25-30 deal with the twin revelation of the Father and the Son to those to whom God has graciously shown them. In vv. 25-30, however, there are three sections that build upon one another. Verses 25-26 are a thanksgiving for God's work in concealing and revealing "these things"—probably a reference to perceiving correctly the meaning of the ministry of Jesus. Verse 27 is a soliloquy about the mutual knowledge of the Father and the Son, and, in turn, those "to whom the Son chooses to reveal him." Finally,

vv. 28-30 are Christ's appeal to all who are "weary" to take his light "yoke" and to learn from him.

Significance. There is a striking, profound, logical sequence to the material in this lesson that should be instructive for preaching: First, on our own, we humans more often than not fail to comprehend God's emissaries and God's purposes (vv. 16-19). Second, our gracious God is active in the world revealing the person of Christ and the purposes of his will to those who live without making pretentious claims to God's favor (vv. 25-26). Third, God's self-revelation transpires freely and graciously through Jesus Christ, who himself is in a special position to know and reveal the person and will of God (v. 27). Fourth, Jesus Christ calls "all . . . that are weary" to "take [his] yoke" and to "learn from [him]." This is a call to admission of our limitations, to acceptance of his authority, and to the full-fledged discipleship of service (vv. 28-30).

This logic can inform the preacher without the sermon being reduced to the level of propositional revelation. The logic of this lesson invites contemplation and conversation between the text and ourselves. Perhaps in relation to the positive elements of the logic, we should formulate and wrestle with a series of questions. For the first item: How and why do we often misperceive the presence and purpose of God in the world around us? Where can we see God at work in our world? What does God call us to do? For the second item: How are we "the wise and the intelligent" rather than "infants" before God? Here, it is helpful to recognize that the contrast is not between sophistication and naiveté, for ancients did not think of children as wonderful little dears but as bundles of chaos who were loathsome and needed to be tamed. Small children were without anything to commend them for acceptance. Thus the issue is pretentiousness. How do we approach God, presuming upon God's grace? For the third item: What can we learn from Jesus' own teaching about God? How do our assumptions about God misinform us? What kind of God does Jesus reveal? How does this challenge our theology and what difference does the God of Jesus Christ make for our living? For the fourth item: What are our human limitations, especially as they cause us to misperceive God and Christ? What is the yoke of Christ—what is the style of living to which he calls us? What kind of disciples are we?

What evidence of Christ's yoke shows in our lives? Does Christ's promise of a light yoke comfort us? challenge us? threaten us?

This passage invites us in our reflection to look at our lives, but not merely so; we are challenged to look at our lives and beyond them, to frame ourselves in the context of God's active presence in the world. An honest exercise in this kind of reflection should help us perceive God with increased clarity, evaluate our lives in terms of how faithfully we are living them in relation to God's will, and hear afresh Christ's challenging call and comforting promise as we are his disciples.

Proper 9: The Celebration

The difficulty confronting preachers and worship planners is the proximity of the Fourth of July to this Sunday and the resulting questions arising about the relation of the Church and its liturgy to civil religion and its rituals. There are two answers at opposite ends of the issue. On the one side, we can say that church-state separation should never be more obvious in America than in churches on Sunday morning when God's faithful gather to remember that "our citizenship is in heaven" (Phil. 3:20), and so we can afford to ignore the occasion altogether. On the other side, we can affirm that ours is a nation under God, intentionally established to be a city set on a hill to shed the beneficent light of Christianity upon the world, and that we owe thanks and obedience to the God whose "love divine hath led us in the past" and by whom "in this free land our lot is cast." Most of us will probably fall somewhere between these two poles, not caring for either ecclesial ghettoism or civic manifest destiny. What, then, to do if we wish to affirm that the Christian has a responsibility toward the state?

Two ideas readily present themselves out of the propers for today. First, from the Old Testament lesson, the commentator says "that all of the characters have a heroic role in this narrative," and speaks of what it means for each of the characters to be involved in trying to discern the will of God in their situations. It may be here that real Christian citizenship is to be found: We serve the nation best when we struggle with the primary issue of serving God. Second, the epistle provides an opportunity to distinguish between the freedom that Paul is talking about (see commentary) and the popular ideas about freedom that are often only an excuse for self-indulgence and greed. What does it mean to be "the land of the free," according to Paul's definition?

The liturgy on this day should be carefully planned so that it does not look like a political rally. As an inappropriate example, in one church the scouts were honored, followed by the veterans, a flag presented from the congressional office, followed by thirty minutes of patriotic war poetry, concerning God's deliverance from our enemies, read by a young woman dressed as the Statue of Liberty. Such national occasions can provide the worship committee with an opportunity to discuss the the significance and symbolism of having flags (civic or ecclesiastical) in the chancel and carried in procession. Do they compete with the central symbol of the faith, the cross? Should churches (denominations) have flags at all? Is the presence of the national flag an unconscious copying of a European state-church pattern that is not appropriate in the American setting? How are flags different from banners?

The intercessions today should include petitions for the nation: the people at large and the various branches of government. The placement of hymns should proceed carefully. The opening hymn should clearly be addressed to God, not the nation.

Proper Ten Sunday Between July 10 and 16 Inclusive

Old Testament Texts

Genesis 25:19-34 is the story of the birth of Jacob and Esau. Psalm 119:105-112 praises divine instruction.

The Lesson: *Genesis 25:19-34*

A Story Without Heroes

Setting. The Old Testament lesson for this Sunday begins a four week series of lessons from the stories of Jacob in Genesis 25:19–36:43. In the present form of Genesis, the cycle of stories about Jacob can be interpreted as continuing the divine promise of progeny that was introduced in Genesis 12:1-4*a* and that provided organization to the stories of Abraham and Isaac. Thus there is unity in Genesis around the theme of the divine promise of progeny, but we must also see that new motifs are introduced as different ancestral figures become the central characters. Even though Jacob carries on the divine promise, he is not Abraham. He is not an ideal of faith, and the account of his birth makes this point clear at the outset. This is a story without heroes. The demonstration of this conclusion will be the central focus of interpretation.

An additional introductory word is necessary for interpreting the Jacob cycle of stories, which is the power of names in the context of the ancient Near East. The giving of names is a rather arbitrary activity in our present culture. The names Sally, Suzy, Bob, or Tom are often chosen by parents because of their sound or because of an important relative who bears the name. The name Tom or Thomas, for example, is not chosen because parents intuit a fundamental predisposition toward "doubting" in an infant boy, which is the meaning of the name. Yet this example is closer to the ancient Near Eastern understanding of the power of names, where the naming of an individual embodies their most fundamental character. In other words, for an ancient Israelite, you are what you are named. Genesis 25:19-34 is written with such an understanding of names. It is a story about naming the quality of characters.

Structure. Genesis 25:19-34 functions as the introduction to the Jacob cycle of stories that continues through Genesis 36:43. These verses contain a variety of different types of literature, which include a genealogy in v. 19, a poem in v. 23, three naming aetiologies in vv. 25 (Esau), 26 (Jacob) and 30 (Edom), and narrative. When we stitch the different kinds of literature together, we have a story that separates into two main parts, which can be outlined in the following manner.

I. Isaac's Genealogy and Rebekah's Infertility (vv. 19-21*a*)
II. The Conflict of Fertility (vv. 21*b*-34)
   A. In the womb of Rebekah (vv. 21*b*-23)
   B. In the birth of the twins (vv. 24-26)
   C. In their early childhood (vv. 27-28)
   D. As adults (vv. 29-34)

Significance. Two matters require commentary. The first is the structure of the story with its tension over fertility and infertility. The second is the importance of names as a commentary on the characters.

The structure of the story is determined by the larger theme of progeny that runs throughout Genesis. God has promised that Abraham would be a great nation. This promise creates two kinds of conflict in the book of Genesis. The first problem is that the matriarchs are frequently infertile, which is more of a theological problem in Genesis than a biological one. It raises the question of what God is going to do about this obstacle to the fulfillment of the divine promise. The introduction to the Jacob cycle introduces this problem by juxtaposing fertility (the genealogy of Abraham) to Rebekah's infertility. The second problem concerns fertility. That is, once God answers prayer in Genesis through the birth of children it creates its own set of problems. In the case of Abraham, it was two sons where the elder was not the son of Abraham's wife, but of his handmaiden. In the case of Isaac, it is two sons born of the same woman. It is as though the momentary crisis of infertility provides the context to address a more severe problem, namely that the divine promise is too potent. The birth of twins creates a conflict of fertility in Genesis 25:19-34, for it raises the question of which one will continue the divine promise to Abraham. As the outline indicates, this conflict between the twins goes through four cycles—from the womb of Rebekah into their adulthood.

The naming of characters is important to the story. An examination of the four stages of conflict between the twins will illustrate the meaning of their names. First, almost immediately after being told that Rebekah is pregnant, the reader learns that it is a problematic pregnancy because the fetuses are in conflict with each other. The divine oracle in v. 23 interprets this conflict for Rebekah. The twins represent two nations and, she is told, that the natural order of things is being disrupted in her womb, because the elder will, in the end, serve the younger. The divine oracle sets up expectations that predispose the reader in favor of the younger child. This one is, after all, the divinely chosen one. Second, the conflict is carried into the birth of the sons, and it is explained in their naming. The first born is red and hairy; he is named Esau. The name *Esau* may mean hairy, while his redness signifies the people who will come from him—namely, the Edomites (which is similar to the Hebrew word for red). The birth of Esau is uneventful. What is surprising, however, is the birth of the second son—the one to whom the reader has already been favorably predisposed. In v. 26 we learn that the second is born grabbing the heel of the first born. The imagery here is not positive, rather it is of the second son trying to reverse the natural order of birth, since all inheritance went to the first. This action of "grabbing by the heel" embodies the character of the second born and thus becomes his name, Jacob, which in Hebrew means, "he who grabs by the heel," or "he who supplants." The third section illustrates how the conflict of the twins permeates the entire family with Isaac favoring Esau and Rebekah, Jacob. Finally, the closing scene illustrates how the twins live out their names. That Esau would give up his birthright (which in Hebrew is built off the word for "blessing") for red pottage (both words in Hebrew are spelled very similarly to "Edom") is a commentary on his rash and impulsive character. That Jacob would trick Esau out of his birthright at a moment when he was vulnerable and famished is also a commentary on his inherently unethical character. This is a story without heroes.

The naming of the twins is important for it is commentary on their character. Furthermore, it is the naming of Jacob that is really central to the story and not the naming of Esau, and he should be the focus for preaching. In focusing on the development of the character of Jacob, it becomes clear that he is a disappointment. The divine oracle to Rebekah about his dominance has set up expectations in the reader about his character, namely that if God has chosen the younger over the elder, then the younger must really be something. As we learn within a few verses, nothing could be further from the truth. In terms of moral development, it would appear that the younger is worse than the elder. And this surprising reversal is the point of the story. The story about Jacob being chosen over Esau is not a story about divine destiny, it is a story about divine grace. It is a story in which Israel looks at herself in the mirror and at the people around her and concludes, "But for the grace of God there I go." It is a story that underscores how there is nothing inherent in the people of God to account for the gift of salvation. The God of Jacob is a God of grace. Paul understands this in Romans 7:15-25*a* when he laments how he is incapable of doing any good without the help of God.

The Response: Psalm 119:105-112

In Praise of Torah

Setting. Psalm 119 is an enormous psalm consisting of 176 verses. Its literary construction is like Gothic architecture in complexity. The psalm is acrostic, but instead of having every line begin with a letter of the Hebrew alphabet, in Psalm 119 each letter of the alphabet controls eight lines. Furthermore, each eight-line section tends to repeat a set cluster of words associated with law as the word of God. The repetition motifs for law provides the thematic unity to the piece, which could be characterized as an anthology both celebrating and teaching the value of Torah. Psalm 119:105-112 is the section controlled by the letter *n* in Hebrew.

Structure. Such a variety of speech forms occurs in these few verses that it is difficult to structure the unit. The forms include praise (v. 105), oath (v. 106), lament (v. 107), and dedication (v. 108).

Significance. The mixture of language, especially praise and complaint or lament, provides the point of departure for interpreting this section. Determining how the modes of speech related in this section will provide guidelines on how this psalm might be used in worship. Psalm 119:105-112 is predominantly about praise for divine instruction. God's word is like a lantern (v. 105), to which the psalmist is unwavering in his or her commitment (v. 106). The language of lament (v. 107) and even potential persecution (vv. 110, 115) never really becomes the object of the psalm. Instead their dangers enhance the psalmist's devotion to Torah. Thus in the end this psalm of confidence in Torah is meant to teach how it is able to provide light and life in a variety of situations.

New Testament Texts

The readings from Romans and Matthew continue, and this week we come to two striking texts: Paul's reflections on life in the Spirit and Jesus' so-called parable of the sower.

The Epistle: *Romans 8:1-11*

Free Life in the Spirit

Setting. Romans 8:6-11 was the New Testament lesson for the Fifth Sunday in Lent in Year A. The following commentary is in part a repetition of the entry for that Sunday.

This passage is part of the larger section of chapters 5–8. As we recognized in considering earlier portions of this section of Romans,

Paul's main focus here is on the life of the Christian community in its experience of God's grace.

Structure. Romans 8:1-17 forms a thought unit on "life in the Spirit." Verses 1-2 are a kind of thesis statement, which summarize earlier passages and point toward an overt statement about the Spirit. Verses 3-11 are a two-part elaboration on the thesis of vv. 1-2. First, vv. 3-8 explain the thesis, as is indicated by the opening word, "For. . . ." Second, vv. 9-11 juxtapose a remark to the statements in vv. 3-8 ("But . . ."). Finally, vv. 12-17 issue a series of conclusions ("So then . . . for . . . for . . . for . . . and if. . . . ").

Significance. The opening verses, 1-5, create a contrast between the inability of the law to produce salvation on the one hand and God's achievement of salvation for humanity by sending the Son on the other. The idea of a "saving sending" is one of the ways in which Judaism spoke of God's gifts of the law and wisdom as acts whereby God moved for the salvation, understood as well-being, of the children of Abraham. Paul (and perhaps other early Christians before him and certainly other early Christians after him) picked up this pattern and used it to express the profound meaning of the saving work of God in sending Jesus Christ. In sending the Son, God has accomplished what the law could not achieve. God has defeated sin and freed humanity to live freely "in the Spirit," under the gracious leadership of the Spirit. These verses create a conceptual background of freedom from sin and freedom for a free walk in the Spirit. With this contrast made, Paul moves on. In preaching this passage, one should give some attention to contrasting our lives prior to Christ with our lives "in Christ."

In vv. 6-8 the apostle does not lapse into Platonic dualism. Rather he uses the antinomic language of apocalyptic eschatology to contrast spheres of power. *Flesh* for Paul can, and sometimes does, mean the real physical human self; but when set against *Spirit* Paul employs the word metaphorically to designate powers other than and often in conflict with the power of God. Paul says to invest your confidence in any power other than God is to choose that which indeed is impotent. It is a bad investment, leading to bankruptcy rather than security; or, to use Paul's own language, death rather than life and peace. Looking anywhere other than to God for one's true security necessarily causes a separation from God, which means that one is at enmity with God. Paul's point: Don't put your trust in anything other than God. One immediately wonders, Who would knowingly turn to anyone or anything other than God as a source of ultimate security? Answer: We all do, all the time! Paul does not address this problem here, but some attention to this topic in the course of preaching this text would be very helpful.

In vv. 9-11 Paul's remarks become more positive in character. He declares who we, as believers, are—we are in the Spirit, and the Spirit is in us. This is the distinguishing mark of the Christian. Paul's turn here is deliberate. With all the previous admonition to set our minds on the Spirit rather than the flesh, we might easily but mistakenly conclude that our salvation is merely a matter of making the right decisions. We do, however, have the responsibility to orient our lives toward God, but the good news of the gospel is that not only are we called to be in the context of the Spirit, but the gracious gift of God to us is the Spirit dwelling in us. Here is the mystery of salvation. We grasp for God because God has already grasped us. Indeed, we are renewed internally as well as externally. The mind-boggling nature of the mystery of grace is seen in the comforting but confusing cluster of phrases Paul uses in vv. 9-11: "in the Spirit"; "the Spirit of God dwells in you"; "the Spirit of Christ"; "Christ is in you"; "the Spirit of the One who raised Jesus from the dead dwells in you . . . his Spirit dwells in you." It is finally impossible to make clear, rational sense of the collection of phrases, but what seems plain is that the division between humanity and the presence and power of God has been eliminated through God's work in Jesus Christ, especially as we know that work in the power of God, which raised Jesus from the grave. In the Resurrection of Jesus, we perceive the presence and the power of God that has now grasped us in order to bathe us in saving grace.

The Gospel: *Matthew 13:1-9, 18-23*

The Parable of the . . .

Setting. The third section of Matthew's presentation of the ministry of Jesus (11:2–13:53) takes a clear turn in 13:1-2 to present some of the material preserved from Jesus' teaching. In the story, Jesus is apparently in Galilee, specifically in a boat on "the sea." Matthew is not overly concerned with the specifics of geography, so a more precise location is not possible or necessary. More important is that the teaching in Matthew, done in the form of parables, follows the controversies in chapters 11–12, which ends with Jesus' statement about his true family. Having said, "Here are my mother and my brothers! For whoever does the will of my Father in heaven is my brother and sister and mother," Jesus teaches and draws crowds of people, some of whom are being formed into the very family of God by the words and work of Jesus.

Structure. There are two large parts to the lesson, vv. 1-9 and vv. 18-23. Generally, the first nine verses present the parable of the sower and the other six verses provide the interpretation of the parable. Between these clearly related units 13:10-17 gives Matthew's version of Jesus' words about the purpose of the parables. In the first part of our lesson, vv. 1-3*a* provide an introduction to the parable per se in vv. 3*b*-9. Verses 18-23 are a step-by-step explanation of the elements of the parable. The explanation treats the parable as an allegory, certainly one type of parable, but not the only kind Jesus spoke, even in Matthew 13. For preaching and worship, vv. 1-9 may be used with or without vv. 18-23.

Significance. This parable occurs in Mark (4:3-8), Luke (8:5-8), and the Gospel of Thomas (82:3-13), as well as in Matthew. Scholars are often concerned with identifying or reconstructing the "original" form of the parable, but for preaching, we are concerned with the text as it is in the canon. This does not mean that investigations into the "pre-Gospel" forms of the parable are irrelevant; rather, the insights of such critical studies are best appropriated for teaching and Bible study, though they may inform the preacher to a degree. Yet, one must be aware of the temptation to preach a text that is in no text and that is not the text of the lesson when one works with historical-critical scholarship on the parables.

What is this parable "about"? The sower. The seeds. The soils. Failure versus success. Scholars suggest each of these as keys to the depths of the parable. If the parable is about the sower, it is essentially christological and points to the role of Jesus in bringing the kingdom of God among humanity. If the parable is about the seeds, then it is a lesson about contrasting kinds of faith, several of which are futile and one of which is real. If the parable is about the soils, it teaches about the responsibility we have in hearing the message of Jesus. If the parable is about failure versus success, it contrasts the initial mixed reception of the gospel with the eventual advent of the Kingdom, the poor beginning belies the fantastic ending.

Perhaps the inability of interpreters to identify "what the parable is about" is the best indicator that this parable cannot be reduced validly to any one of these levels. The allegory provides a fixed interpretation of the parable, and perhaps some will find that a secure guide to interpretation. But, if we dare, the story may throw open a series of windows on a variety of fields related to our faith. Thus preaching the parable from a variety of points of view may communicate the dynamic quality of this powerful story, looking now at Christ, then at faith, then at responsibility, and then at the marvelous richness of the Kingdom that triumphs despite setbacks. There may well be other central elements in this parable that will be suggestive for brooding over this text. Certainly preachers will not need to explore the side streets of this parable in detail, for there is more than enough crucial imagery and thought in this passage to keep even the most gifted pulpiteer busy. It is striking how the parable proceeds slowly and rhythmically telling of the first three sowings, which ultimately fail; but when the fourth sowing and its results are described, the language and the form of the story explode. Trying to capture that "energy pattern" in the sermon would be an appropriate challenge.

Proper 10: The Celebration

Today's epistle prompts the suggestion that the unabridged Cranmerian General Confession be used in today's liturgy. For those who, after more than two decades of liturgical revision, may no longer be able to find a copy of the pristine version, we reproduce it here.

Almighty and most merciful Father,
we have erred and strayed from thy ways like lost sheep.
We have followed too much the devices and desires of our own hearts.

> We have offended against thy holy laws.
> We have left undone those things which we ought to have done,
> and we have done those things which we ought not to have done,
> and there is no health in us.
> But thou, O Lord, have mercy upon us, miserable offenders.
> Spare thou those, O God, who confess their faults.
> Restore thou those who are penitent,
> according to thy promises declared unto mankind
> in Christ Jesus our Lord.
> And grant, O most merciful Father, for his sake,
> that we may hereafter live a godly, righteous, and sober life,
> to the glory of thy holy Name. (From *The Book of Common Prayer,* [New York: Thomas Nelson and Sons, 1935] p. 8.)

Where this prayer has been kept in use, "no health in us" and "miserable offenders" have vanished. The compilers of the Revised Common Lectionary have included the scriptural warrant for these phrases in today's epistle, for at no point does it show up in the Roman cycle. We observe that the language of the prayer is considered archaic or offensive in the culture among the same folk who lustily sing, "Amazing grace, how sweet the sound,/ That saved a wretch like me." Yet "miserable" means to be wretched and pitiable, whether we are aware of being in that state or not. Self-consciousness has nothing to do with it. Liturgy should make us aware of reality, not protect us from it. Paul knows his wretchedness in today's epistle. Jacob doesn't, but that makes him no less a miserable human being. Other hymns that are appropriate commentary on the epistle are "Dear Master, in Whose Life I See" and "Thou Hidden Love of God, Whose Height."

This is the only Sunday in which the parable of the sower appears in the lectionary; the parallels are not used in Years B and C, so the preacher may opt to deal with it primarily. The emphasis should be on the amazing yield that God's planting produces, not on chastising the bad soils! For, miserable as we are, it is only by God's grace that we are not unfertile soil.

Proper Eleven Sunday Between July 17 and 23 Inclusive

Old Testament Texts

Genesis 28:10-19*a* is the story of Jacob's dream at Bethel in which he sees a ladder extending from heaven to earth, receives the divine promise of progeny, and then responds to it, while Psalm 139:1-12, 23-24 is a confession about the breadth of God's presence, which extends from the depths of Sheol to the heights of the heavens.

The Lesson: *Genesis 28:10-19*a

Putting Conditions on Visions

Setting. This is the second lesson from the Jacob cycle. The trickster Jacob has been living out the meaning of his name for some time now. He has not only tricked his brother, Esau, out of his birthright, but he has also stolen Isaac's blessing that rightfully belonged to Esau. (The blessing is an almost magical gift of prosperity which can only be given once.) In the present story Jacob is on the lam, fleeing from his brother Esau, who, as you might imagine, is rather upset with him, for what Jacob tried to do during Rebekah's labor—namely, grab his brother by the heel and reverse their order of birth—has now been accomplished through other devious methods. Jacob's ultimate destination is Haran where Rebekah's kinsman Laban resides, but in Genesis 28 he is still traveling and thus is forced unknowingly to spend the night at a sacred place, which provides the setting for a dream-vision from God.

Structure. The account of Jacob at Bethel separates nicely into three parts, which include an introduction providing the setting of the dream (vv. 10-12), a divine speech (vv. 13-15), and a response by Jacob (vv. 16-22). Jacob's speech does not end at v. 19*a* where he names the location of his dream, Bethel (House of God), but he continues on to present a vow in vv. 20-22. By cutting Jacob's speech in half we actually skew the interpretation of this text in the larger cycle of the Jacob stories.

- I. Introduction (vv. 10-12)
  - A. Flight of Jacob from Beersheba to Haran
  - B. Time: evening
  - C. Jacob's dream of a ladder
- II. The Divine Speech (vv. 13-15)
  - A. Identification of God
  - B. Divine promise
    - 1. Land
    - 2. Descendants
    - 3. Divine presence
    - 4. Guaranteed return
- III. Jacob's Response
  - A. Recognition of divine presence and the naming of Bethel
  - B. Conditional vow

Significance. The story is two-sided. It illustrates how God is following through the divine promise to Abraham and Sarah, and how Jacob tries to supplant God by putting conditions on God's promise. A brief commentary on the outline will illustrate these points.

First, the setting of the story in vv. 10-12. Jacob's dream at Bethel is the first of two theophanies (appearances of God) that provide the central pegs of the story of Jacob. The second theophanic story is Jacob's struggle with God at the Jabbok River in Genesis 32, which will be the lectionary reading in two weeks. These two theophany stories share many similarities. Each story takes place at night, and in each, Jacob unknowingly enters a place where he will be confronted by God. The point of these similarities is that Jacob is not presented to us as a character who is out looking for God. In fact the opposite is more to the point—namely, that God is out looking for him.

Second, the divine speech in vv. 13-15. God enters Jacob's world through a dream and then proceeds to address him in a lengthy speech that repeats the blessing of progeny which has been a unifying theme throughout the story of the ancestors in Genesis. Much of the speech is a verbatim repetition from other promises like Genesis 12:1-4*a*, and includes such elements as the gift of land, of descendants, and of being a universal blessing. The divine promise to Jacob goes on, however, and includes additional elements in v. 15 that are worth noting. At the close of the speech, God promises to be with Jacob throughout his travels and to bring him back to Canaan safely. These additions sound like icing on the cake of what is already a series of spectacular promises, but they end with the somewhat unsettling comment that God will not leave Jacob alone until these promises are in fact fulfilled. When one recalls that Jacob was not really looking for God in the first place and that he is not exactly an ethical ideal, one wonders whether these closing words are a divine promise or threat.

Third, Jacob's response in vv. 16-22. Jacob makes two speeches after his dream. In the first speech, he comments on the holiness of the place and how he did not know it before his dream. He ends this speech by naming the site, Bethel (House of God). In the second speech, Jacob responds to the divine promises. This speech provides insight into the character of Jacob, because his vow, that the God of his parents would also be his own God, does not qualify as one of the great statements of faith in Scripture. Instead, it is hedged with no less than five conditions. The Lord will indeed be Jacob's God if (1) God stays with him, (2) protects him in his travels, (3) gives him food, (4) provides clothing, and (5) brings him back to Canaan in peace. In this response, Jacob is negotiating a deal more than he is demonstrating how the life of faith is one of risk. Jacob is not living out the promise to Abraham at this point. Instead, his response illustrates how he is still living out the character of his name, only this time he is trying to grab God by the heel when putting conditions on his vision.

God promised in v. 15 not to leave Jacob until he had executed the full dimensions of his promise. Certainly the story line must be heading for a confrontation, because it is difficult to see at this juncture how Jacob could be a blessing to anybody, much less all the nations of the world. His only demonstrated talent up to this point has been to steal blessings for his own self-preservation. Thus the story would appear to have two main points that could be probed in preaching this text. One, God is doggedly pursuing Jacob, and the reason for it is certainly not his character. Rather, it is because God is obligated to promises. This side of the story provides insight into the nature of divine grace. God frequently acts because God is not free to do otherwise. The second point has to do with Jacob and how his limitations are frequently our own. He cannot yet see clearly the vision of his own dream at Bethel, because this vision is blurred by his own self-interests. Thus we begin to suspect that he is headed for a character transformation, if he is ever going to embody the divine promise.

The Response: *Psalm 139:1-12, 23-24*

The Hound of Heaven

Setting. Psalm 139 is difficult to classify. It has elements of the hymn, but the psalmist also wants to teach about the searching presence of God. The focus of hymnic praise and wisdom teaching shifts gears in vv. 19-24, where the psalm of lament takes over.

Structure. Psalm 139 separates into two parts. Verses 1-18 focus on praise and teaching, while vv. 19-24 shift to lament. The lectionary retained two of the three subsections in the first half of the psalm (vv. 1-6, 7-12), while in the second section it has eliminated the language of lament in vv. 19-22 but retained the conclusion in vv. 23-24. The result is a psalm of praise and teaching that is devoid of any lamenting.

Significance. The lectionary psalm separates into three parts. In vv. 1-6, the psalmist has submitted to the powerful searching eye of God. The language in this section is personal, as the psalmist outlines the ways in which God is continually present. Verses 7-12 are less personal even though the language remains in the first person. Here the psalmist makes larger conclusions about the power of God to be present in all places and in all situations, which have the effect of teaching. Verses 23-24 become more personal again in tone as the psalmist concludes by requesting still further examination by God. As the psalm is presently structured, it critically evaluates the Old

Testament lesson, since these words could not possibly be Jacob's at this point in his story. Thus by using this psalm in the worship setting, the congregation must be aware that they are moving ahead of the central character in the lesson, since the psalm removes all conditions between the psalmist and God.

New Testament Texts

The Romans learn of the distinction between the flesh and the Spirit, and how the Spirit endures by the grace of God. In Matthew we explore the distinctions between weeds and wheat, and how the wheat endures despite the presence of weeds in this world. The readings point to the grace (Romans) and the sovereignty (Matthew) of God. In different ways both texts ponder the significance of these grand theological themes for the lives of believers.

The Epistle: *Romans 8:12-25*

Life in the Spirit

Setting. Within the larger section of Romans 5–8, the eighth chapter is itself a nearly self-contained unity with clearly identifiable parts. Generally this chapter is a meditation on the nature and significance of Christian life. It is crucial to notice two items. First, this section "ends" Paul's long reflection of the operation of grace in chapters 5–8. Second, this beautiful, hopeful meditation immediately precedes the following agonizing section of Romans, chapters 9–11, which will wrestle with the fate of Israel in the working of God's grace.

Structure. Chapter 8 is neatly structured. Verses 1-11 take up the theme of Christian life as life in the Spirit. Then, vv. 12-17 employ the metaphors of sonship (obscured in the NRSV) and childhood (preserved and amplified to take in sonship) to reflect upon the significance of our relationship to God. Next, vv. 18-30 bring a strong eschatological cast to Paul's thought by speaking of future freedom and glory. Finally, vv. 31-39 conclude this section by declaring that the ultimate destiny of Christian life should be victory through "the love of God in Christ Jesus our Lord." The reading should be extended beyond vv. 18-25 to include vv. 26-30, which cohere and find meaning together despite the paragraphing of the NRSV and other translations that break vv. 18-30 into two or more paragraphs.

Significance. Following Paul closely through the careful sections of chapter 8, especially vv. 12-30, is not easy work. The opening words, "So then," let us know that Paul is drawing conclusions from the previous verses where he made the clear positive point that Christian life is life in the Spirit, not life in the flesh or under the law of sin. Verses 12-17 explain the theme ("because") of vv. 1-11. To paraphrase: Christian life is life in the Spirit because persons led by the Spirit are the children of God. In one way Paul is speaking about Christian identity or self-understanding (more communal than individual, though there are implications for individuals), but he goes on to speak about the significance of such life. Life in the Spirit is much more than an identity; it is a relationship to God that has come as a gift from God. For now, the distance between (sinful) humanity and (righteous) God is overcome as God adopts us as God's children. And Paul continues that since we are now God's children, we will be heirs. This expansion of the metaphor accomplishes at least two things: (1) It introduces a profound eschatological cast to the meditation—we are experiencing grace, and there is more to come! (2) It translates Christian suffering into meaningful suffering. If we are co-heirs with Christ, Paul says our suffering for Christ (he is not talking about routine health or financial problems) is like Christ's own suffering—that is, an anticipation of the glory to which God will bring us.

With the ideas of life, the Spirit, relationship to God, eschatology, Christ, and suffering before the Romans, Paul speeds up his argument by moving into a new gear in vv. 18-30. Now Paul's topic is life in the Spirit as a life of hope. Paul has been focused on the community of Roman (and other?) Christians in vv. 1-17; but now his vision of the operation of grace through the work of the Spirit becomes cosmic in scope. This passage is difficult, because we are not adept at thinking in such cosmic terms, and we are not really accustomed to reflecting upon the need of creation for redemption. Yet, Paul believes with deep conviction that the very fabric of creation is itself, like humankind, captive to the corrupting power of sin, so that creation, or the cosmos, is at odds with God.

Paul, however, also believes and states that "the creation itself will be set free from its bondage to decay and will obtain the freedom of the glory of the children of God." In Paul's vision of God's work of redemption, humanity and the cosmos are intricately related to each other. The fate of the one is the fate of the other. Why? Because humanity and the cosmos have in common that they are creations, created by the one creator God. The hope of all creation is in the faithful Creator who did not abandon a sin-trapped creation but who, in Jesus Christ, reclaimed and thoroughly identified with all of creation. Thus Paul can make the bold statement in vv. 28-30.

The Gospel: *Matthew 13:24-30, 36-43*

God's Somewhat Mysterious Ways

Setting. The literary context is essentially the same as that observed for last Sunday's lesson. This parable, long called "the parable of the wheat and the tares" from the language of the King James Version, follows the allegorical explanation of the parable of the sower. Again, Matthew provides an allegorical explanation for this parable in vv. 36-43. Between parable and explanation there are two other parables and a note about Jesus' consistent use of parable for teaching the crowds.

Structure. This parable is a busy text with characters coming and going amidst work, treachery, conversation, decision making, and pronouncement. The explanation defines the meaning of selected characters and actions in the sequence of their occurrence in the parable. The explanation adds an element to the items recognized in the parable, when in v. 43 Jesus prophesies the good fate of the righteous and calls for those with ears to hear to listen.

Significance. In one way Matthew provides extensive interpretive aid for understanding this parable. First, Jesus tells us that the parable is about the kingdom of heaven. Second, the disciples name the parable: "the parable of the weeds of the field." And, third, we hear an allegorical interpretation of the parable straight from the mouth of Jesus. But this parable is not pure allegory, for even the interpretation given in vv. 36-43 deals only with selected elements:

Sower	=	Son of Man
field	=	world
good seed	=	children of the kingdom
weeds	=	children of the evil one
enemy	=	devil
harvest	=	end of age
reapers	=	angels

Moreover, elements of the parable that Jesus does not explain are at least as interesting as those which he does. What is the point of enmity between the farmer and his enemy? Why this particular kind of nocturnal sabotage? Since all farmers hoe and weed, why the odd farming practices? How, then, is this parable about the kingdom of heaven, or cutting through the circumlocution, how is this parable about God?

Remarkably this parable wrestles with the age-old problem of suffering. Why are there weeds? Why do bad things happen to good people, and why does a good God allow terrible things to happen? Equally remarkably, this parable makes little effort to answer these very real and very troubling questions. We wonder about evil, as do the servants in this parable, "Master, did you not sow good seed in your field? Where, then, did these weeds come from?" The question is real. But listen to the answer, "An enemy has done this." What does the answer tell us? That God is not ultimately responsible for the evil in this world. The answer provides us with no more precise information, though the words of the allegorical explanation name the enemy, "the devil." This is not dualism, but it is the blunt recognition of the existence of evil and the reality of the conflict between God and evil that pollutes the world in which we live. Do we de-mythologize or re-mythologize this text? Not if we follow the lead of the parable, which recognizes the reality and leaves it rather a mystery. Instead, the parable reasserts the goodness of God in eschatological terms. We have the rich imagery and language of apocalyptic judgment in the explanation, but to become obsessed with that would be to get sidetracked. The parable tells us both that God is not the author of evil and that God knows the difference between what is good and bad, right and wrong, the children of the evil one and the children of the Kingdom. Moreover, the parable tells us that although we wish God would hurry up and get rid of the weeds, God acts knowingly and ultimately for our well-being. This is a remarkable point. God's knowledge and power are not challenged but are affirmed, and evil is not turned into a divinely provided opportunity to improve our moral character.

The parable does many things. It distinguishes God and evil and takes both seriously. It tells us that God recognizes the difference between good and evil, does not approve of the evil, and intends to take care of the problem at the appropriate time. Although this message may not suit everyone, it offers hope and even beckons persons to identify with God's ways. The hope to which this parable leads us is more than the purely negative hope of looking forward to the elimination of evil. Rather, the allegorical interpretation steers us to the positive dimensions of the text, "Then the righteous will shine like the sun in the kingdom of their Father." In the context of that hope we hear, "Let anyone with ears listen!" Theology, hope, and challenge are the themes of this dynamic lesson. May the sermon find the fiber and the force of Jesus' words.

Proper 11: The Celebration

The story of Jacob's ladder has contributed much to Christian hymnody, and so today's Old Testament lesson provides an opportunity for the congregation to discover how one Bible story has informed our worship. Obviously, the African American spiritual "We Are Climbing Jacob's Ladder" comes immediately to mind. In the liturgy it may serve as an introduction or response to prayer, or a response to the dismissal and blessing at the end of the service. "Nearer, My God, to Thee" may be the best known hymn based on this story, although today's congregations may not know enough about the Bible to make the connection. This gives the preacher a chance to do a teaching sermon in relation to the hymn and thus save the hymn from what has become its funeral connotations.

Summertime is frequently a time for congregations to enjoy singing in the gospel hymn tradition, and it is important to remember that many of those hymns were based on the assumption that the singers understood the scriptural references, as in "Nearer, My God, to Thee." In the same way, the second stanza of "Blessed Assurance, Jesus Is Mine" refers to the Jacob story in its line "Angels descending, bring from above / Echoes of mercy, whispers of love." The intensely personal character of the hymn corresponds to the character of Jacob in any case!

Most congregations are familiar with the hymn "Beneath the Cross of Jesus," but they do not know an additional stanza that refers to Jacob's ladder. It could be printed in the bulletin to be inserted before the final stanza.

O safe and happy shelter,
  O refuge tried and sweet,
O trysting-place where heaven's love
  And heaven's justice meet!
As to the exiled patriarch
  That wondrous dream was given,
So seems my Savior's cross to me
  A ladder up to heaven.

An excellent opening for this day is the following, which can be sung to any standard common meter tune, such as Dundee.

O God of Bethel, by whose hand
  Thy people still are fed;
Who through this earthly pilgrimage
  Hast all thine Israel led:

Our vows, our prayers, we now present
  Before thy throne of grace:
Great God of Jacob, be the God
  Of each succeeding race.

Through each perplexing path of life
  Our wandering footsteps guide;
Give us each day our daily bread,
  And raiment fit provide.

O spread thy covering wings around,
  Till all our wanderings cease,
And at our Father's loved abode
  Our souls arrive in peace.

To thee as to our Covenant-God
  Our whole selves we'll resign;
And this not as a tithe alone,
  For all we have is thine.

Responses to the epistle and preparations for the Gospel might be any of the following:

(a) Stanza 5 of "And Can It Be that I Should Gain," beginning "No condemnation now I dread."

(b) The following Wesley stanza, to the tune St. Michael or St. Thomas:

O come and dwell in me,
Spirit of power within,
  And bring the glorious liberty
From sorrow, fear, and sin.

(c) The hymn, "Come Down, O Love Divine."

Proper Twelve
Sunday Between July 24 and 30 Inclusive

Old Testament Texts

Genesis 29:15-30 is a story of reversals, of how the trickster Jacob is tricked by Laban, while Psalm 105 is a song of praise that celebrates God's deeds as evidence of the fulfilled promises that are made in the covenant with Jacob's children.

The Lesson: *Genesis 29:15-30*

Whom Is God Watching?

Setting. The third reading from the Jacob cycle locates Jacob in Haran with Rebekah's kinsman Laban. God, however, is absent in this story. There are neither divine speeches as in the first story in Genesis 25:19-34, nor any divine promises of salvation through a dream theophany as in Genesis 28:10-22. Instead, Genesis 29:15-30 is a story that looks closely at the action of the two central characters, Jacob and Laban, and the consequences of their actions. The absence of God raises a central question—namely, whether God sees this action at all and, if so, what is it that God sees?

Structure. Although the lectionary text ends at v. 28, the present outline will extend through v. 30, while the commentary will also include v. 31. The story of Jacob and Laban separates into three parts.

I. The Marriage Contract (vv. 15-20)
II. The Trick (vv. 21-29)
III. The Victim (v. 30)

Significance. Two aspects of Genesis 29:15-30 require commentary. The first is how the confrontation between Jacob and Laban is a story of reversals, especially of how Jacob falls prey to a better trickster. The second issue is to determine where, if any place, we are to locate God in this story, since an answer to this question will provide an avenue for interpretation and preaching.

First, Genesis 29:15-30 is a story of reversals, and as such it provides a new beginning to the Jacob cycle. The story of Jacob began with the problem of twins, which was presented in the following manner. Initially Rebekah is pregnant with male twins. The plot developed in such a way that the older Esau was the natural choice, but this order was subverted by the younger Jacob. Thus in the opening scenes of the Jacob cycle, Jacob is the trickster. The present story picks up many of the same dynamics, but reverses them. Instead of Rebekah, we have her kinsman Laban. He, too, has a problem with children and inheritance, but it is two daughters rather than two sons. The plot develops in such a way that the younger Rachel is the natural choice of Jacob, but through Laban's trick, this choice is subverted so that Jacob ends up marrying the older Leah. In the end, Jacob is the one tricked instead of the trickster. When we view the story from the point of view of these reversals, the tricking of Jacob by Laban is an example of our hero getting a taste of his own medicine. It is a story that was probably told with great humor, for in it ancient Israelites were poking fun at themselves.

The story also has a theological dimension, which comes to the foreground when we broaden our focus beyond Jacob and Laban and ask who is the victim in the trick. Jacob is certainly a victim and this point is highlighted through the many reversals outlined above. But the absence of God in the confrontation between Jacob and Laban would suggest that we should not be encouraged to make more out of this confrontation than we already have. God does not appear to take sides in the confrontation of the two tricksters, and instead stays away from the story altogether. God does enter the story, however, in Genesis 29:31, and even though it goes beyond the boundaries of the lectionary text, it provides another level of commentary on how we are meant to read this text. When we broaden the scope of interpretation, what has been lurking beneath the surface of the Laban and Jacob confrontation rises to the surface—namely, the fate of Leah in the trick. The primary victim in the confrontation of the tricksters is Leah. When God does enter the story in v. 31, it is only she that merits divine attention, for Leah was a pawn in a trick that was not her choosing, and she is now condemned to a life of hatred.

Genesis 29:31 reads, "When the Lord saw that Leah was hated, he opened her womb." This verse indicates whom God was watching during Laban's trick through the motif of divine blessing. Blessing has been a unifying motif throughout the Jacob stories. Jacob stole Isaac's blessing from Esau (the magical word of prosperity), and God promised Jacob divine blessing at Bethel. Both in the Jacob cycle and throughout the ancestral stories, this motif embodies fertility. Thus it is important to note that when God does enter the narrative in v. 31, it is Leah who embodies the blessing of God and gives birth to several sons.

The divine attention and blessing bestowed upon Leah suggests that in many ways the confrontation of Jacob and Laban is her story. She is the innocent victim of the trick, and because of that, she is also the only one worthy of God's attention and blessing. In this role she parallels the situation of Hagar in relation to Abraham and Sarah that was the lectionary text for Proper Seven (Genesis 21:8-21).

The Response: *Psalm 105:1-11, 45*b *or 128*

Celebrating God's Blessing

(The lectionary provides alternative psalms for this Sunday. The following commentary is on Psalm 128. See Proper 14 for commentary on Psalm 105.)

Setting. Psalm 128 is usually characterized as a Wisdom Psalm. It begins with the wisdom saying or maxim in v. 1, which almost sounds like a beatitude from the gospel of Matthew. This beatitude is followed by two addresses that encourage the worshiper to embody the qualities of fear or reverence that were praised in the opening verse.

Structure. Psalm 128 can be separated into three parts: the beatitude in v. 1, a priestly address to the worshiper in vv. 2-4, and a divine blessing in vv. 5-6. The psalm can be outlined in the following manner.

I. Encouragement to Fear God (v. 1)
II. Result of Fearing God (vv. 2-4)
  A. Meaningfulness of labor (v. 2)
  B. Rich marriage (v. 3*a*)
  C. Many children (v. 3*b*)
  D. Summary (v. 4)
III. Divine blessing from Zion (vv. 5-6)

Significance. The central motif in Psalm 128 is the "fear of God." It occurs in v. 1 and then again in v. 4. Fear of God is not a psychological attitude, thus it cannot be reduced to a pious disposition. Rather, fear of God is a view of the world coupled with a life-style that is fashioned in the light of it. Verse 1 makes this very clear by paralleling the "fear of God" with the motif of "walking" in God's ways. This couplet underscores that fear of God must entail certain kinds of action, or, as we say in contemporary theology, praxis. Verses 2-4 outline the results of being a God-fearer. The psalmist describes how a life-style fashioned in God will be meaningful. Three things are specifically mentioned, yet the last two (marriage and children) are interrelated: labor will not be reduced to meaningless toil, nor will marriage. Verses 5-6 shift the focus from the individual worshiper to the collective in order to bestow a divine blessing upon all of Israel.

When Psalm 128 is read as commentary on Genesis 29 it has two meanings. First, it critically evaluates the actions of Jacob and Laban, for neither of these characters is yet fashioning a life-style out of God's promise of blessing. Thus neither is able to embody a blessing for others. Second, it also provides positive commentary on Leah's situation, as one who embodies the divine blessing that is being idealized in vv. 2-4. This second reading underscores how Psalm 128 must not be read simply as an illustration of rewards theology—namely, the understanding that belief in God guarantees a good life or getting what one wants. Even though she embodies divine blessing (symbolized through her frequent births) and indeed sees the reality of God in her ability to give birth (symbolized through the naming of her children), her life situation is certainly not one to be envied. Leah illustrates how fashioning a life-style out of fear of God also redefines what are our notions of reward in this life.

New Testament Texts

These verses from Romans are magnificent and they bring this portion of Paul's letter to a conclusion with a declaration of God's sovereignty. Sovereignty finds meaning here as Paul speaks of the security of believers who are bathed in God's supreme love. The text in Matthew takes in a broad sweep of material, all of which challenges us to rethink and reorient our priorities in relation to God; for encountering God motivates us to put God (and God's ways) above all else.

The Epistle: *Romans 8:26-39*

God's Love Prevails!

Setting. Readers may turn to Proper 11 for discussion of the setting of this week's epistle lesson.

Structure. Verses 26-30 are actually the last part of the section 8:18-30, but the verses serve in this lesson to declare a theme that is the point of departure for the meditation in vv. 31-39. Verses 26-28 make a strong statement about what we usually term the sovereignty of God, and, then, vv. 29-30 form a chain-like statement that declares, more than explains, what God's sovereignty means for believers. In turn, vv. 31-35 pose a series of rhetorical questions meant to provide further elucidation by eliminating certain misinterpretations and establishing by implication the correct understanding of Paul's teaching. Verse 36 quotes Psalm 44;23 to give an Old Testament precedent for Paul's pronouncements; and, then, vv. 37-39 move into the indicative to declare boldly what was stated in vv. 26-30 and implied in vv. 31-35.

Significance. Verses 26-30 speak of two of the most difficult doctrines for many contemporary Christians, sovereignty and predestination. Over the years Christians have developed questions in relation to these beliefs for which they often have not found adequate answers. Does God play favorites? Why doesn't a good God do more in relation to the whole of humanity? On what basis—other than whim—does God foreknow and predestine (or foreordain)? Are such doctrines still plausible?

Perhaps it will be no final answer to these difficult questions, but it is crucial to notice not only what Paul's statements are but also what Paul's statements are not. Paul is not doing systematic theology in this passage. While he is elaborating on the theological themes that we have noticed, he is not making full-blown statements of the meanings of these matters; rather, he is declaring them. His purpose is not to illuminate or to educate the Romans, but to inspire or assure them. Recognizing this motive and hearing this tone in Paul's statements helps one to know how to approach the passage for preaching. These verses impart a bold word of assurance concerning the power, purposes, and dependability of God. Christians are given a certitude for living. Paul portrays a very active God with these lines. The chain of activities—called, foreknew, predestined, called, justified, glorified—recognizes God's deliberateness, intervention, and direction in relation to humans. Examination of the chain shows that Paul is not laying out a system. There is little intelligible difference between the Greek words translated "to foreknow" and "to predestine," and strangely the idea of believers being called occurs twice and functions in different lines. In v. 28 being called is the result of God's purpose. Then, after the intervening statement in v. 29, we read in v. 30 that the calling is added to God's predestination and, in turn, that justification and glorification are added to the calling. The statements are genuinely compatible but recognizably distinct. This shows that Paul is talking in a swirl of language about the operation of the love of God, not so much teaching as preaching—speaking more for inspiration than didactic purposes. Thus we may put perfectly logical questions to this passage that the text cannot possibly answer.

Paul's point in the subsequent section (vv. 31-39) is quite simple: God's love has grasped believers in such a way that there is absolutely no one and nothing that can come between God and the believers. Paul introduces a wide range of images of cosmic power in these verses: death, life, angels, rulers, things present, things to come, height, depth, or anything else in all creation. One key to this beautiful passage is in the phrase "anything else in all creation." Recall that Paul believes creation is marred by the power of sin, but God's power has defeated that force in the death and Resurrection of Jesus Christ. The Creator has been and is at work for the redemption of creation, so that no creaturely thing can defeat God by dominating other creatures (humans) to God's exclusion. This text hits one of the high notes of faith.

The Gospel: *Matthew 13:31-33, 44-52*

Treasure New and Old

Setting. The setting is essentially the same as that discussed for Proper Ten. For this Sunday, we encounter five or six additional brief parables.

Structure. Verses 31-33 preserve the parables of the mustard seed and the yeast, two so-called "small to large" parables. Then, vv. 44-50 record, in rapid order, the parables of the hidden treasure, the pearl, and the net, three "kingdom" parables. Next, v. 51 asks about the disciples' comprehension of the parables, before v. 52 concludes the lesson (and this section of Matthew's Gospel) with a saying about "every scribe who has been trained for the kingdom of heaven." The lesson actually holds three separable parts together (vv. 31-33, 44-50, 51-52). The possibilities for preaching are many. One could profitably focus on either vv. 31-33 or 44-50, or one could easily work with only one of the parables from either section or even with the saying in v. 52.

Significance. We often assume when we encounter parables that if we can successfully reconstruct the original setting in which a parable was spoken that we will have a key to how and when to preach these texts. But the Synoptic Gospels frequently frame and aim the same parables differently, so our assumption may not be a valid one. Or, better, the goal of finding the original setting may be an impossible one. Perhaps, then, we should look within the individual parables or at the clusters of parables for internal clues about the intention of the text(s).

One normally reads that the parables of the mustard seed and the yeast are comparisons of small, unpretentious, or inauspicious beginnings with the final large, impressive, or awesome results. Thus the parables are taken to contrast the coming of the Kingdom in the modest ministry of Jesus with the great final form that the Kingdom will take in God's good time. But the images in the text make this interpretation questionable, for both the mustard plant and yeast were common negative images in first-century Judaism. Mustard plants were nothing but despised weeds, and yeast was the item actually, physically cleaned out of the house before Passover, lest it leaven and thereby corrupt the unleavened bread of the celebration. So, in what direction do the parables themselves point us? Probably toward the defiance of expectations. What you see is not what you expect, and it won't fit neatly with normal piety. Thus our religious assumptions are challenged by the negative force of these images. In brief, the Kingdom may offend us!

In turn, the parables of the hidden treasure and the pearl both underscore that some things demand our all. Such is the Kingdom, which requires us to arrange our priorities, so that all that we have and all that we are, are oriented toward God's reality or will. These parables teach about Christian responsibility, saying that nothing short of everything is required of us by God.

The parable of the net is actually a loose allegory on final judgment. This parable is similar in structure and tone to that of the wheat and the tares in 13:24-30. Indeed, these two parables frame the material between them and give to everything a strong eschatological cast. Judgment is inevitable, and our situation is urgent. Jesus' call to responsibility in relation to God's will and work is not to be taken lightly, for there are real consequences to the way we orient our lives toward God.

The issue of understanding, which began the parable discourse in 13:10-17, now comes to the fore a second time, creating another frame around Matthew's material. Then, Matthew gives us Jesus' saying about the scribe trained for the Kingdom. Remarkably the order of the householder's bringing goods from his treasure reverses the normal manner of stating things: new and old, not old and new. The fresh takes priority over the preserved. This image is both fitting for Jesus himself as he lived and worked and for those who hear his call to discipleship. Jesus taught that truly vital faith is current and forward looking, it is not merely zeal for the status quo, although it is not necessarily iconoclasm.

Proper 12: The Celebration

Christopher Webber's *A New Metrical Psalter,* published by the Church Hymnal Corporation, is recommended for those who would like to use the psalms as standard hymns. The translations are not forced so as to be amusing to the modern ear, as much of the old Scottish Psalter now is, and they are all in common, long, or short meter, so that they can be easily sung to tunes already known by the congregation. The volume also gives permission for one time reprinting by churches in church bulletins.

Psalm 128, one of the options for today, is also appropriate for use at a wedding. The Presbyterian Hymnal also has a contemporary metrical translation by Dwyn M. Mounger, "How Happy Is Each Child of God." Its language is more egalitarian.

The epistle suggests the use of the following text by James Montgomery. It is not familiar in America, but is easily sung to the short meter tune, St. Thomas ("Love Thy Kingdom, Lord."). The words make it a particularly fine opening hymn and are a reminder that every Lord's Day is also a celebration of Pentecost (see Introduction).

Lord God the Holy Ghost,
  In this accepted hour,
As on the day of Pentecost,
  Descend in all thy power.

We meet with one accord
  In our appointed place,
And wait the promise of our Lord,
  The Spirit of all grace.

The young, the old, inspire
  With wisdom from above;
And gives us hearts and tongues of fire,
  To pray and praise and love.

Spirit of light, explore
  And chase our gloom away,

With luster shining more and more
  Unto the perfect day.

Spirit of truth, be thou
  In life and death our guide;
O Spirit of adoption, now
  May we be sanctified.

The Old Testament lesson suggests the following confession of sin:

M: Let us confess our sins before God and one another. [silent recollection]
M: For those times we have actively deceived others for our own benefit:
P: We ask forgiveness, Lord.
M: For those times we have participated in the deceits of silence:
P: We ask forgiveness, Lord.
M: For the injuries our deceits have inflicted upon the innocent:
P: We ask forgiveness, Lord.
M: May the Spirit put to death the selfishness in each of us, help us to know ourselves forgiven and to live as children of God.
P: Amen.

Obviously, this prayer will be most appropriate either after the reading of the Old Testament lesson or after a sermon that has dealt with that lesson if the allusions are to have meaning. The last petition is based upon the epistle.

Proper Thirteen
Sunday Between July 31 and August 6 Inclusive

Old Testament Texts

Genesis 32:22-31 is the account of Jacob's fight with God at the Jabbok River, while Psalm 17:1-9, 15 is a psalm of lament that ends with words of confidence.

The Lesson: *Genesis 32:22-31*

A Story of Transformation

Setting. An interpretation of Jacob's struggle with God at the Jabbok River requires that we look briefly at the larger context of the Jacob cycle and return to a topic that was introduced in the opening lesson on the Jacob cycle—namely, the power of names in the shaping of the stories.

First, the context. The Jacob cycle can be viewed as a large repetition of stories. We noted last week how the struggle between Jacob and Laban presented a repetition and reversal of many of the motifs that were present in the opening story. Repetition can be viewed on an even larger scale in the Jacob stories, which could be diagramed in the following series of conflicts.

Genesis 25–27	28	29–31	32	33–36
(Birth/Canaan)	(Bethel)	(Haran)	(Peniel)	(Return/Canaan)
Jacob	God	Jacob	God	Jacob
Esau	Jacob	Laban	Jacob	Esau

The diagram illustrates how the story of Jacob encompasses three conflicts: Jacob and Esau, God and Jacob, and Jacob and Laban. The conflict between Jacob and Laban is between two similar characters, and it stands at the center of the Jacob stories. The conflict between Jacob and Esau frames the entire Jacob cycle. This repetition raises the question of whether Jacob will be different at the end of the story than he was at the beginning. The two encounters between God and Jacob are pivotal to the Jacob cycle because whatever transformation may take place in the character of Jacob must occur in these stories. Two weeks ago we saw that very little change occurred in Jacob at Bethel, and that this foreshadowed an inevitable conflict between himself and God. The story of Jacob's struggle with God at the Jabbok River is the setting in which this conflict will be played out. It is the climax of the Jacob stories because it occurs in the larger context of Jacob preparing to meet Esau. The question of whether Jacob will ever become anything more than a trickster must now be answered once and for all. This question, however, has as much to do with God and God's salvation as it does with Jacob.

Second, the power of names in the Jacob cycle. In the commentary on Genesis 25:19-34 (Year A, Proper 10), we noted how the names of individuals in ancient Israel embodied their most fundamental character. Thus the stories of Jacob up to this point have really been a series of commentaries on his name, "one who grabs by the heel." The importance of naming will resurface on two levels in Jacob's struggle with God at the Jabbok River. First, it will designate a transformation of character in Jacob as he is renamed "Israel" by God. Second, the power of naming will also be explored in relation to God, and this is a new element in the Jacob cycle. People in the ancient Near East (including Israel) believed that what was true about the naming of persons was also true about the gods. Thus the name of a god embodied the fundamental character of that god, and thus to possess the name of a god was to have access to the power of that god. In other words, names had power not only over individuals, but also over gods. An example of this belief is evident in the Babylonian creation mythology, *Enuma Elish*. This mythology celebrates the creative power of Marduk, the central deity of the Babylonians, and it ends by giving a list of fifty of his names. The point of this list is twofold: one, the names embody the different kinds of power that Marduk possesses; and, two, possession of these names by the worshiper provides direct access to the god, Marduk. The significance of divine names is also central to Genesis 32:22-31, because at a crucial point in the struggle at the Jabbok River Jacob asks for God's name and is denied it.

Structure. The larger context of Genesis 32 provides important background for interpreting vv. 22-31. The imagery of a divine army in v. 1 foreshadows the impending confrontation between Jacob and God, but Jacob's vision of God is blurred in vv. 2-8 because of his fear of Esau and his army of four hundred men. Jacob has two responses to this situation. First, he prays to God in vv. 9-12 and in so doing misquotes the divine promise to his own advantage when he states twice that God promised to "do him good." In Genesis 31:3 God promised to be with Jacob and not necessarily to do him good as Jacob would interpret it. Second, he sends gifts to Esau in vv. 13-21 in the hope of appeasing his brother's anger. Genesis 32:22-31 separates into the following three parts.

I. Introductory Setting (vv. 22-24)
  A. Place: Jabbok River
  B. Time: evening
II. The Struggle (vv. 25-29)
  A. Divine attack (vv. 25-27)
  B. Struggle over names (vv. 28-29)
III. Concluding Setting (vv. 30-31)
  A. Place: Peniel (v. 30)
  B. Time: daybreak (v. 31)

Significance. The central section of Genesis 32:22-31, vv. 25-29, is a story of transformation that is inaugurated by a divine attack. The struggle and eventual transformation of Jacob occurs in two parts. First, God subtly slips into the story in v. 25, and the night-long fight that ensues is in many ways a recapitulation of the story of Jacob up to this point. Jacob, "the one who grabs by the heel," is strong, so strong that he can withstand God and survive. Realizing this he tries to coerce a blessing from God in v. 26. The second part of the struggle shifts to a more fundamental level, when God asks Jacob what his name is in v. 29. Jacob states his name and in so doing gives God access to the core of his character. God takes it and reshapes it into Israel, "one who struggles with God." The change of name and a new physical weakness mark the initial transformation in Jacob/Israel. His inability to gain access to God's name signifies the second stage of transformation in his character, for it marks a limitation between himself and God. Prior to this Jacob made treaties with God (Genesis 28) and Laban (Genesis 31) as an equal partner on his own terms. In the present struggle, however, the giving of his name without having God reciprocate signifies a new vulnerability in his character (or perhaps the ability of God also to be a trickster for the sake of salvation). In either case, this new limitation in Jacob/Israel's character provides the setting for his final transformation through the divine blessing in v. 29.

The transformation in Jacob/Israel is reinforced by the contrast between the opening and closing setting to the story, for what had been the Jabbok River the evening before becomes Peniel ("The face of God") the following morning. Thus geography and setting reinforce the transformation in character. This transformation of character is carried over into Jacob's meeting with Esau in Genesis 33:10-11, where he states that his gifts are no longer an attempt to appease Esau in order to save his own life, but simply a sharing with Esau of his own experience of God's grace. With this confession the Jacob cycle is essentially completed.

The Response: *Psalm 17:1-7, 15*

A Morning Prayer for Protection

Setting. Psalm 17 pleads for protection. The references to testing in the evening (v. 3) and of the psalmist awakening in the morning (v. 15) suggest that this is a morning prayer for protection.

Structure. Psalm 17 separates into three sections: vv. 1-5 include a prayer petition (vv. 1-2) and a description of the innocence of the psalmist (vv. 3-5), vv. 6-12 include another prayer petition (vv. 6-9) and a description of the enemies of the psalmist (vv. 10-12), and finally, vv. 13-15 include an appeal for divine judgment (vv. 13-14) and a closing confession (v. 15) by the psalmist. The lectionary reading includes verses from each of these three sections, but the selection of the verses—especially with their emphasis on petition (vv. 1-2, 6-9) and confession (v. 15)—results in a much narrower scope to the psalm, so that it is read as a confrontation between God and the psalmist. The abridged lectionary reading of this psalm can be outlined in the following manner.

I. Petition with Statement of Innocence (vv. 1-5)
   A. Petition (vv. 1-2)
   B. Statement of innocence (vv. 3-5)
II. Petition with Statement of Confidence (vv. 6-9, 15)
   A. Petition (vv. 6-9)
   B. Statement of confidence (v. 15)

Significance. The abridged form of Psalm 17 provides commentary on Jacob's struggle with God at the Jabbok River, especially if we read it as his morning song. The motifs of a night visit by God (v. 3) and of a morning recognition that the psalmist has seen the face of God (v. 15) provide direct connections to Genesis 32:22-31.

The preacher also has opportunity to reflect on the times when God is adversary or enemy. Several other psalms (for example, 13; 44:23-26) wrestle with God's oppressive absence, as do the prophets who feel tormented by God as they protest the loneliness (for example, the confessions of Jeremiah) of their mission.

New Testament Texts

The lesson from Romans moves on to declare God's faithfulness toward Israel (chapters 9–11), and the Gospel reading comes from the early portion of the fourth section of Matthew, with special focus on Jesus as founder of the forming Church.

The Epistle: *Romans 9:1-5*

Anguish Over Israel and Affirmation of God

Setting. Following Paul's meditation on grace in Romans 5–8, we encounter the apostle's difficult and anguished deliberation in Romans 9–11. These chapters are often referred to as Paul's statement on the fate of Israel, but his reflections, at their core, are more theological than anthropological, so that a better way to think of this section of the letter is to name it Paul's meditation on the faithfulness of God in relation to humanity, especially Israel. The verses of the lesson open this section with very personal remarks from Paul.

Structure. These five verses more-or-less unwind in an unsystematic manner. Paul begins this new section of the letter rather abruptly and quite enigmatically in vv. 1-2 by speaking of the deep anguish he experiences. Then, he states the cause for the distress in v. 3. In turn, vv. 4-5 list some of the prerogatives that the Israelites had experienced, the last of which was that the Christ came from them. Having mentioned the Messiah, Paul pronounces a kind of Jewish doxology and declares the "amen" in affirmation of God's working with Israel.

Significance. Paul begins abruptly a new section, which takes one of many directions that could have come out of the meditation in chapters 5–8. But he does not randomly come to this reflection on God's relationship to Israel. As early as 3:1-8 Paul had touched on this theme, and now, after the extensive reflections on God's grace (from which the apostle assures the Roman Christians that they cannot be separated), he returns to consider how God is related to his chosen people, the Israelites. Paul begins his remarks by locating himself "in Christ"—that is, in the context of God's saving power as it has been established in and through the person and the work of Jesus Christ. Paul realizes that he is secure in Christ; thus he practically puts himself under oath to make a statement that he knows is in fact an impossibility. Paul's love and concern for his own people, God's chosen people, Israel, is so great that could he be removed from Christ so that they could themselves be found in the context of Christ, he would become accursed in their behalf. This statement shows indeed that Paul had not turned sour on his own people, and as this larger section (Romans 9–11) unfolds, we learn that ultimately Paul does not believe that God has reneged on the choice of Israel, though at the moment of his writing Paul recognizes that many of the Israelites are outside the context of God's saving grace in Jesus Christ.

Having named the cause of his anguish and having stated his own impossible solution to the crisis of Israel's lack of faith, Paul turns to the story of God's dealings with Israel and recalls the central moments of that history. The particulars of Paul's list are interesting, but one should not get lost looking at the trees. Rather, the end of the path Paul takes, not the scenery along the way, is the point to which the apostle directs us. God brought forth the Christ from Israel, and that is both Israel's greatest privilege and Israel's greatest hope. The coming forth of Christ is not merely one item among many in Israel's favored past; for Christ does not belong to the past. He came, but more importantly God has set him "over all" so that he is (though Paul does not use this language in this passage) Lord. The position of Christ over all is humanity's hope, as it is Israel's hope. God who blessed Israel abundantly in the past is at work in and through the exalted Christ so that "salvation has come to the Gentiles" (11:11), and in turn "all Israel will be saved" (11:26). For Paul, the current crisis confronting Israel is a cause of great pain and distress, but Paul's faith in the faithfulness of God allows him, despite his personal agony, to break out in praise of God and, then, to affirm boldly ("amen") God's work.

The Gospel: *Matthew 14:13-21*

Christ Shows the Degree of God's Grace

Setting. The fourth major section of Matthew's presentation of Jesus' ministry begins at 13:54 and continues through 19:1 or 2. In this section, Jesus steadily withdraws from the high level of public interaction that characterized his ministry through the first three sections of Matthew's account. He turns deliberately toward his smaller band of disciples to form them into a basic community of faith. The initial story in this fourth section gives the motivation for his alteration: Jesus is rejected outright when he returns to minister in Nazareth. This rejection forebodes and symbolizes the forthcoming rejection of Jesus, that brings him to the cross. Furthermore, we learn in the report of Herod's taking interest in Jesus (14:1-2) and of the concern of the governing authorities over Jesus' activities. This story gives urgency to the situation and starts the clock toward the time when the powers-that-were would move to eliminate Jesus altogether. Following the report of the burial of the Baptist (14:3-12) we come to our lesson, the story of the feeding of the five thousand, with the clues of the foregoing materials that the moment is a crucial time.

Structure. This deceptively simple story is indeed complex and has at least five parts: (1) Jesus hears of the death of John and withdraws by himself to a deserted place (14:13*a*); (2) the crowds follow Jesus and he has compassion and heals the sick (14:13*b*-14); (3) at evening the disciples and Jesus discuss feeding the crowd, and although the disciples initiated the conversation, Jesus has the final word (14:15-18); (4) Jesus takes charge and acts (14:19); and (5) the results—distribution, consumption, satisfaction, and profusion despite the size of the crowd.

A "standard" ancient miracle story comprised three elements. First, the problem was recognized; second, some action produced extraordinary results; and third, confirmation of the results was offered. Our story modifies and elaborates the typical form for a miracle. Before the miracle, we learn of Jesus' reaction to John's death. Then, we hear about the crowd and Jesus' compassion. The problem is not narrated, rather a two-round exchange between the disciples and Jesus sets up the situation. The report of the action taken by Jesus contains many striking but unnecessary details, and the confirmation is dual: The crowd was filled, and there were twelve baskets of leftovers among the large crowd.

Significance. This story is almost infinitely rich in content and detail, so that the preacher draws back in fear lest something crucial be ignored! The story is simply too good to be true or, better, too good not to be true! Explanations that approach this text on the level of sheer history can never grasp its meaning. Certainly some moment in the ministry of Jesus lies behind this text, but in preserving the moment and retelling the story, Matthew and other early Christians (compare the parallel versions in the other Gospels) told the story so that it became a vehicle for nearly the full freight of God's good news. Matthew's version is as much a statement about the person of Jesus and the nature of the life of the Church as anything. Older rationalizing interpretations fall flat when suggesting that the crowd had food up their sleeves or in their pockets (as first-century Jews traveling away from home often did), which they were unwilling to share with others until they witnessed and were moved by Jesus' own generosity. This story is not merely an admonition to "be good." The story is more about Jesus (somewhat in contrast to others) than about human beings. Examination of the details of the narrative find the repeated christological pointers.

Initially in the lesson, we learn of Jesus' being informed of John's death. Moved by this news, Jesus seeks to withdraw alone to a deserted place. This is the same kind of place where he was tempted at the outset of his ministry. Moreover, this was the kind of place where Israel wandered for forty years, sustained by manna from heaven. In spite of Jesus' desires and efforts to get away, the crowds follow and seemingly prevent him from achieving the desired solitude. Yet, when he views the crowd, Matthew tells us that he had compassion; and the deep caring was more than passive. Jesus healed the sick. If Jesus is supposed to look a lot like God in this story—as God's Son—then, we learn that we cannot wear God down with our problems, and we cannot exhaust God's gracious power.

The disciples confront Jesus with still another problem, the lack of food. (The story gives no indication the disciples had or thought the crowd had food stashed away.) Jesus turns the problem of the crowd into a problem for the disciples! Jesus' followers are given the responsibility for attending to the real needs of others. But at this point, they don't have the wherewithal to minister. So Jesus takes charge. He gives the disciples an order—they are to bring what they have to Jesus. And that too is part of what it means to be a disciple.

With the little bit of food in hand, Jesus continues to take charge. He orders the crowds to be seated on the green grass. The information that the grass was green may simply be superfluous, but it may be a gateway for homiletical imagination. The greenness in the "deserted place" underscores the lushness of life in Jesus' presence. But this is a pointer, not a point. The real action takes place as Jesus turns to God. The power for the work Jesus is about to do comes from God. It flows from God to Jesus and, in turn, through Jesus to the disciples, who extend the results of God's abundant grace to those in need. Thus our work as Christians is ultimately God's work. And the thanks we speak for all life's unspeakable riches is thanks to God, from whom all blessings flow. And, in the end, we are assured that God's provisions are more than enough for our needs.

Proper 13: The Celebration

Today's Old Testament lesson is the source for what many consider to be Charles Wesley's greatest hymn, "Come, O Thou Traveler

Unknown.'' Isaac Watts said that one hymn was worth all of his own works together. The poem sees the story as analogous to our wrestling with God and discovering in the encounter the redemptive person of Christ. All fourteen stanzas are too much for a contemporary congregation, but the preacher would do well to seek nourishment from them on a regular basis in preparation for preaching on this passage. The complete poem may be found in *The United Methodist Hymnal* (No. 387). Four stanzas for congregational use are at No. 386 in *UMH* and at No. 638 in the 1982 Episcopal hymnal. The Episcopal version has altered the text at two points and so is less desirable.

American Methodists have traditionally sung this hymn to a Scottish melody, which in their hymnals they have named after their own Bishop Candler for whom the text and tune was a great favorite. It is not as widely known as it deserves, and care should be taken about introducing it so as not to prejudice the congregation with an unfamiliar text and tune. The tune might be used as an organ or piano voluntary for several weeks in succession. Also for several weeks prior to use by the congregation a solo voice might use the following stanza as a response to the absolution:

> Tis Love! 'tis Love! Thou diedst for me,
> I hear thy whisper in my heart.
> The morning breaks, the shadows flee,
> pure Universal Love thou art.
> To me, to all, thy mercies move;
> thy nature and thy name is Love.

Preachers should not overlook the significance of the Old Testament lesson and the epistle happening to fall on the same Sunday, since Paul in effect is discussing the covenant with Israel who receives his name in the wrestling narrative.

Today's Gospel can provide the scriptural warrant for the celebration of the Lord's Supper in those congregations where it is not a weekly event and where the pastor is trying to decide when to have the summer observance. In this text we are told of one of the meals of Jesus that informs our understanding of the Lord's Supper (as opposed to the Last Supper). We see here the same actions of taking, blessing, breaking, and giving that characterized all of the dominical meals. These hallmarks can be used to discuss Christ's action in the local church's midst as the preacher applies the symbolic acts to Christian life. We give of what we have, express our gratitude, identify with the suffering of Christ in the broken bread and poured wine, and give ourselves as bread for the world as Christ has given himself for us. In relation to the theme of the epistle (God's faithfulness to persevere, or Israel's lack of faith), the preacher may wish to explore the significance for Matthew of having twelve baskets left over.

Proper Fourteen Sunday Between August 7 and 13 Inclusive

Old Testament Texts

The Old Testament texts explore the power of God in history. Genesis 37 introduces the story of Joseph and Psalm 105 reviews Israel's entire history of salvation.

The Lesson: *Genesis 37:1-4, 12-36*

The Power of Oppression

Setting. The Old Testament lessons for the next two Sundays come from the story of Joseph. The story of Joseph in Genesis 37–50 provides a hinge between the preceding ancestral stories of Abraham and Sarah-Hagar, Isaac and Rebekah, and Jacob and Rachel-Leah (Genesis 12-36), and Israel's subsequent slavery in Egypt (Exodus). The stories of Joseph, therefore, must be read with an eye on what has preceded and what is to follow—on the preceding theme of the ancestral promise and on the subsequent theme of the Egyptian oppression. The two lessons from the Joseph stories will allow us to examine each of these themes. In the first lesson, the sale of Joseph into slavery in Genesis 37, foreshadows the Egyptian oppression, but complicates this theme because the oppressors here are his own brothers and not the Egyptian pharaoh. In the second lesson, Joseph's interpretation of God's hand within the events of his life in Genesis 45 links his story back to the earlier divine promise to the ancestors by showing how God's hand was at work throughout his life. When both stories are read together, they necessarily complicate how we, as

Christians, view actions and events in our world. Genesis 37 cautions us about evaluating people too quickly, for it illustrates how the pharaohs are not the only evil persons in this world. Genesis 45 cautions us about evaluating God too quickly, for this story provides theological interpretation on a series of events that appeared to be running their course independent of God. Genesis 37 is about the power of oppression, and Genesis 45 is about the power of the promise.

Structure. The Old Testament lesson includes the introduction to the Joseph story in Genesis 37:1-4 and the account of how Joseph was sold into slavery by his brothers in vv. 12-36. The lesson does not include Joseph's account of his dreams in vv. 5-11. Our interpretation of the lesson will follow the limits of the lectionary lesson by focusing on the theme of oppression. Yet it should be noted that the dreams of Joseph are central to these stories, and, indeed, the motif of dreaming even reappears in v. 19 when Joseph is described as a "dreamer" by his brothers. The following outline, therefore, will include the account of Joseph's dreams in vv. 5-11.

- I. Joseph the Spoiled Son (vv. 1-4)
  - A. The youngest
  - B. The favorite son
  - C. A tattletale
  - D. He is hated by his brothers so that there is no peace
- II. Joseph the Dreamer (vv. 5-11)
  - A. A dream of power
  - B. A dream of being worshiped
- III. Joseph's Journey into Slavery (vv. 12-36)
  - A. Jacob's command for Joseph to seek the peace of his brothers (vv. 12-17)
  - B. Selling Joseph into slavery (vv. 18-28)
  - C. Telling the lie to Jacob (vv. 29-36)

Significance. Genesis 37 is a dark story of which the central theme is the oppression of Joseph. Joseph's journey into slavery in Egypt is providing an introduction and a transition to the account of Israel's slavery in Egypt. Yet Genesis 37 complicates the story of slavery that will follow in the book of Exodus, because the oppressors in Genesis

37 are not Egyptians but Israelites, Ishmaelites, and Midianites. A look at several of the central motifs in the chapter will illustrate how Genesis 37 is a story that holds up a mirror to the people of God in a search for evil.

Genesis 37 is inundated with family metaphors. The word *brother* (which in Hebrew means "clan" or "kin") occurs no less than twenty times (vv. 2, 4 twice, 5, 8, 9, 10 twice, 11, 12, 13, 14, 16, 17, 19, 23, 26, 27 twice, 30). The centrality of this motif leaves no doubt that this is a story about family. The use of *father* ten times (vv. 1, 2, 4, 10 twice, 11, 12, 22, 32, 35) and *son* eight times (vv. 2, 3, 32, 33, 34, 35 twice, 36) provide still further reinforcement about the narrow and intimate boundaries in which we are meant to read this story. The prominence of these motifs makes it clear that it is within the context of the clan or family that the author wishes to probe the evil effects of oppression.

Inequalities abound in this story. In vv. 1-4 Joseph is introduced as a spoiled child. He receives special clothing from his father. He enjoys a special relationship with Jacob and uses it against his siblings by being a tattletale. Verse 4 ends the introduction with the ominous conclusion that there is no shalom (peace) in this family.

The opening inequalities lead to a radical reversal in vv. 12-36, when the favored son begins a trip into slavery. The story is filled with ironies. It begins in v. 14 with Jacob requesting that Joseph seek the shalom (peace) of his brothers, who are out tending the sheep. (The NRSV translates this verse, "Go now, see if it is well with your brothers" but the Hebrew quite literally reads, "Go now see the peace of your brothers.") The repetition of this motif from v. 4 prepares the reader for anything but peace on this trip. The brothers hatch a plot to kill him, but then a rather confusing scenario develops in which Joseph is thrown into a pit, sold to the Ishmaelites, and perhaps stolen by the Midianites (who then sell Joseph to the Ishmaelites), while Reuben and Judah assume different roles. The story may be a conflation of two different accounts. More important than being able to separate different stories at this point is noticing that emerging from the conflation of stories is a larger group of characters, who are now incorporated into this story of oppression. Not only Israel but also the Ishmaelites and the Midianites are portrayed as willing oppressors.

Both of these groups of people function within the orbit of the Israelite clan. Ishmael is the half-brother of Isaac, while the Midianites are Moses' in-laws.

This story reminds us of the power of evil. Oppression is not a problem "out there" with the Egyptians. Rather it is a problem that can actually begin with the people of God themselves when there is no shalom (peace), and once that happens, it can radiate out to influence others. The abundance of motifs about the family, along with the fact that the central characters are all related (Israelites, Ishmaelites, and Midianites), underscore how evil as well as good can leaven our world. The final verse of the chapter carries the evil to a new level altogether by introducing the character, Pharaoh, who will build on the actions of the brothers by enslaving all of them as told in the book of Exodus.

The Response: *Psalm 105:1-6, (7-15) 16-22, 45*b

A Song of Praise

Setting. Psalm 105 recounts in some detail the salvation history of Israel, from the ancestors to the gift of the land. The central focus or purpose of the psalm is not to recount history or a story, but to praise God for the gift of salvation in the setting of worship. Because of this focus, Psalm 105 is best characterized as song of praise.

Structure. The lectionary reading breaks off after the summary of the Joseph story and provides an option on whether to include the account of the ancestors. The following outline will include all of vv. 1-22.

- I. Introductory Call to Give Thanks (vv. 1-6)
- II. Hymnic Recounting of Salvation History (vv. 7-22)
  - A. God's gift of covenant (vv. 7-11)
  - B. The ancestors (vv. 12-15)
  - C. Joseph (vv. 16-22)
- III. Praise Benediction (v. 45*b*)

Significance. The psalm is significant in its praise to God. This is established forcibly in vv. 1-6 with the frequent commands for the worshiper to give thanks, to call, to make known, to sing, to tell, to give glory, to rejoice, to seek, and to remember. The final command provides the framework for the remainder of the psalm: Remember that the Lord is a God of covenant (vv. 7-11). The remainder of the psalm provides illustration and thus definition of what it means that the Lord is a God of covenant. As commentary on the Joseph story, and particularly the lesson for this Sunday, *covenant* means that God stays with Israel even when they act out of evil motive. This insight provides transition to Joseph's confession in the next lesson.

New Testament Texts

The lesson from Romans moves further into this important portion of Paul's letter (chapters 9–11) by describing the universal promise of salvation. We will continue in this larger section next week. The text from Matthew simply follows on the heels of last week's lesson and continues our reading of the early part of the fourth major division of Matthew's account of Jesus' ministry (13:54–19:2), in which he works on the community that is forming among the disciples.

The Epistle: *Romans 10:5-15*

The Difficulty of Believing That Salvation Is for All

Setting. The lesson comes from Paul's extended and difficult discussion of God's relationship to Israel in the light of the Christ-event (Romans 9–11). At the beginning of Romans 10, Paul states that he desires and prays that those Israelites who currently do not believe the gospel of Jesus Christ may be saved (v. 1). He continues to speak somewhat favorably of the Israelites through vv. 2-3, saying that they are zealous but ignorant, so that they seek to establish their own righteousness rather than to trust God. Then, in v. 4 he says, "For Christ is the end of the law so that there may be righteousness for everyone who believes." Paul's mixed attitude toward the nonbelieving Israelites and his declaration that Christ has made the law obsolete by bringing righteousness through faith lie behind the verses of this week's lesson.

Structure. The form of argumentation in this lesson may seem strange to modern readers. Paul works from the statements made in vv. 1-4, especially in relation to his position that the Israelites ignorantly sought a righteousness of their own rather than the righteousness of God. Some could reply to Paul that Scripture directed the Israelites to do exactly what Paul accuses them of doing in error. Thus Paul engages in a rabbinic style of argumentation that essentially explains away the literal sense of a text and replaces it with another text. In v. 5 Paul states the text that seems to contradict his position (Leviticus 18:5). Then in the following verses he laces together six other passages from the Old Testament (v. 6 = Deuteronomy 9:4 and 30:12; v. 7 = Psalm 107:26; v. 8 = Deuteronomy 30:14; v. 11 = Isaiah 28:16 [already quoted more fully and accurately in Romans 9:33]; and v. 13 = Joel 2:32 [3:5 in Hebrew and the Septuagint]). Paul mixes his own comments and perhaps even an early creed (v. 9 or vv. 9-10) with these lines from the Old Testament. The pattern of the argument is "unfolding"; Paul links one line with another by word or thought association. The outcome is that Paul explains the meaning of Leviticus 18:5 so that Joel 2:32 takes its place. The logic and structure is that of ancient Jewish rhetoric, which may turn out to be more helpful in sermon preparation than one initially suspects.

Significance. Above all, Paul wants to make the point stated in v. 12, "For there is no distinction between Jew and Greek; the same Lord is lord of all and is generous to all who call on him." That is the gospel. But Paul knows that it is possible to object to his proclamation on the basis of Scripture. Thus he argues down the potential objection by going himself, and directing the attention of the Romans, to the very passage that could undermine his message. If Paul can use seemingly conflicting parts of the canon of Scripture to create a dynamic debate, why can't the preacher do the same today? Congregations may even find it stimulating to recognize difficulties in holy writ. But if this line is chosen one should proceed with sensitivity and judiciousness—as Paul did.

If Scripture says both that "the person who does these things [that is the law] will live by them" and that "if you confess with your lips that Jesus is Lord and believe in your heart that God raised him from the dead, you will be saved," what are we to believe? What gives Paul precedence over Moses? We begin by realizing that Paul speaks from the perspective of faith, in the light of the revelation of Christ, and after the cross and Resurrection. Paul takes Christ and God's work in Christ as the standard whereby he finds the meaning of sacred texts. Paul does not attribute to Moses the authority of God. What God did and does in Jesus Christ is the final determining factor for how we are to appropriate Scripture into our lives. And in Christ, God acted to do for humanity what we were and will never be able to do for ourselves, God calls us to faith in Jesus Christ. In so doing God establishes the power of God's own righteousness in our lives. This act of God means that saving grace runs past ethnic and cultic lines and into the hearts of all humankind. In Christ, God eliminated the kinds of human distinctions that once marked groups off from one another. As God in Christ draws us to himself in righteousness, we are drawn to one another in reconciliation. Thus Paul envisions the meaning of salvation along both vertical and horizontal lines on a universal scale. This is a vision worthy of God.

The Gospel: *Matthew 14:22-33*

The Amazing Authority of Jesus Christ

Setting. The general setting for this passage was discussed in the material for last Sunday, so readers may turn to that discussion. For this passage it is also helpful to compare Matthew's version of this mighty act of Jesus with Mark's telling of the story (6:45-52). It is noteworthy that Luke does not include this story in his Gospel, perhaps because the story was difficult even for some first-century believers. In any case, Matthew offers a very rich variation of the story, the details of which are noteworthy as aids for interpretation.

Structure. The passage actually has two major scenes. First, vv. 22-27 are close to Mark's account, telling of Jesus' separation from the disciples, their difficulties at sea because of the weather, Jesus' coming to them across the sea, their fear, and Jesus' revealing word of assurance. Second, Matthew gives us the exchange and the events that transpire as Peter attempts to come across the water to Jesus. This story provides a stronger, more explicit contrast between Jesus and the disciples, especially Peter, than the accounts in Mark and John. The narrative also functions as a vehicle for teaching about the character and the identity of Jesus.

Significance. There are a variety of ways to approach this passage for proclamation. One may elect to focus on either the first or the second scenes of the story, or one may deal with the whole. Whichever path one takes, there are two basic strategies to make the sermon "work." First, avoid getting into the "science" of this story. Past generations of interpreters often gave rationalizing explanations of the account—Jesus was only up to his ankles in shallow water, or Jesus knew where the reef was that ran off the shore just beneath the water and he was walking on top of it, or this is a post-Easter story that was mistakenly placed in the context of Jesus' ministry prior to his death and Resurrection. Such explanations explain away the power of this story and refuse to admit that this story goes beyond what most people are prepared to believe or are able to understand. In the same way, sermons that say, "I don't know whether he walked on the water, but I do know that he calmed the storms of my life," sell short the profundity of this passage. Second, notice how carefully and dramatically Matthew has crafted this story and try to capture some of the brilliance of this account in your own sermon—that is, don't hesitate to preach a powerful and dramatic sermon on this text. And since the story is laden with images and details, turn to art for images and illustrations.

This story is about the authority of Jesus. At several different points and in several different ways Matthew recognizes Jesus' power: Jesus sends the disciples away; Jesus dismisses the crowd; Jesus exercises authority over the elements of nature, both the water and the wind; and Jesus speaks with confidence and power to the disciples. One often reads that this story is cast as a theophany—that is, a bold revelation of the divine; and anyone who turns to Job 9:8; Psalm 107:23-32; and Isaiah 41:4-10; 43:25 will see how deliberately Matthew (and Mark and John) have shaped their telling of this miracle to reflect and pick up the idea of the dramatic self-disclosure of God to humanity. Moreover, Matthew does not leave us wondering about the source of Jesus' amazing authority. After sending away the disciples and the crowds and before we see Jesus walking on the water, Matthew tells us that Jesus went off alone to pray. As Jesus turns away from people who come to him because of his power, he turns to God, the real source of his power, before he comes to those in peril who have need of his saving presence and power.

The second scene of this story implicitly and explicitly contrasts the faith and power of Jesus with the lack of faith and lack of power of the disciples. The disciples are incapable of withstanding the chaotic forces of nature, and when Jesus comes to them, they do not recognize him but fall back in fear, thinking he is a ghost. Silly superstition rules their lives rather than the dynamics of an intimate relationship with God. Jesus prays, but the disciples howl. Jesus draws on the power of God to do what is humanly impossible (forget gurus in India!); but the disciples cower in their own reasonable sense of inadequacy. Yet, in the story one disciple, Peter, starts to believe that Jesus called them to do the things that he did (see 10:1). Thus Peter asks to duplicate what Jesus did, and initially he is able to move like Jesus. But the moment Peter loses sight of Jesus and begins to focus on the chaos, he sinks back into a worse state than he was in when he was in the boat! Yet again he turns to Jesus, "Lord, save me!"; and Jesus does. The story ends with Jesus having rescued not only Peter but also the disciples. And with the wind calmed, the disciples in their rightful awe see clearly who the one they call "Lord" is: He is the Son of God.

Proper 14: The Celebration

Many pastors are away on vacation at this time of year. We are now subject to the guest preacher. Frequently congregations drink deeply of the visitor's vintage years of sermonic production without regard for the current lectionary readings. Or lay members of the congregation, now invited to speak, take advantage of the opportunity to straighten out all the affairs of the church, be the lessons what they may, or the attendance ever so small.

Worship committees should consider planning the preaching schedule far enough in advance to give guests the chance to prepare a sermon based on some portion of the lectionary, if they choose to do so. A letter of invitation might say something like, "It is our practice here for the sermon to be based on one or more of the lessons for the day. On August 8 the lessons will be as follows: Genesis 37:1-4, 12-36 (the story of young Joseph's struggle with his brothers and how they sold him into slavery); Romans 10:5-15 (Paul's great affirmation that salvation is for everybody); and Matthew 14:22-33 (Peter walking on the water). Please let us know if you would like to use one of these, or if you prefer to use another text, let us know which one to substitute (Old Testament, epistle, or Gospel).'' In this way the church performs a teaching function for guest preachers and also observes the practice of reading the lesson that is to be preached rather than reading one set of lessons and preaching from something else. Likewise, preachers invited to other churches can demonstrate the shared ministry of preaching and the ecumenical character of the Church by using the lessons current for the day.

Hymns for today can include for the epistle, ''There's a Wideness in God's Mercy,'' and for the Old Testament and Gospel, ''How Firm a Foundation.'' An emphasis on either the Old Testament or epistle suggests Wesley's ''All Praise to Our Redeeming Lord'' as an opening hymn.

Proper Fifteen Sunday Between August 14 and 20 Inclusive

Old Testament Texts

In Genesis 45, Joseph provides his brothers with a theological interpretation of the events that have befallen him, while Psalm 133 celebrates kinship.

The Lesson: *Genesis 45:4-20*

The Power of the Promise

Setting. Scholars have long since noted how different in character the Joseph stories are from the other ancestral stories. The sharpest point of contrast is the absence of God as a central character in the Joseph stories. God does not appear as a visitor at mealtime, does not talk directly to people, and does not control the direction of events through supernatural intervention. Instead, the scope of the Joseph stories is more narrowly defined on the plane of human interaction within the family and in the larger arena of international relationships. This more narrow focus implies that God is hidden in the Joseph stories, which raises the question of whether he is active at all. Where is the power of the promise to the ancestors in the Joseph stories? This question provides the focus for interpretation.

Structure. A brief description of two different organizing structures is necessary to interpret Genesis 45. First, we observe the important role of dreams in structuring the Joseph story and the placement of Genesis 45 within this structure. Second, we analyze the internal structure of the passage itself.

First, even though God is for the most part hidden in the Joseph stories, the reader suspects divine involvement in the story through Joseph's constant dreaming. It seems as if he cannot help dreaming, and it is his dreams that keep pushing the plot forward. The dreams of Joseph and their fulfillment structure the story into two parts. The larger structure concerns the initial dreams of Joseph in Genesis 37:5-11 concerning his family and the fulfillment of these dreams in Genesis 42–47. Within this larger structure is a smaller cycle of dreams and their fulfillment in Genesis 40–41. These dreams concern the Egyptian butler, the baker, and finally even Pharaoh. The two structures can be illustrated in the following manner.

(37)	(40–41)	(42–47)
Family Dreams	Egyptian Dreams and Their Fulfillment	Fulfillment of Family Dreams

These two structures are interrelated in the larger story because the dreams about Egyptians (and more importantly their fulfillment) in Genesis 40–41 set in motion a series of events that allow for the fulfillment of Joseph's initial dreams concerning his family in Genesis 42–47.

Genesis 42–47 detail the fulfillment of Joseph's dreams concerning his family. This section of narrative progresses in two stages with Genesis 45 providing a hinge: 42–44 [45] 46–47. Genesis 42–44 narrates two trips by Joseph's brothers to Egypt for grain. These stories have an undercurrent of trickery as Joseph toys with his brothers. Genesis 45 is a hinge because in this chapter Joseph discloses his real identity, while also providing a theological interpretation of his brother's earlier treachery toward him. Genesis 46–47 completes the Joseph story by narrating how the family was reunited in Goshen. The analysis illustrates how Genesis 42–47 reverses the family disunity that characterized the opening story in Genesis 37.

Second, the structure of Genesis 45. The movement toward family unity that is evident in the larger structure of the Joseph story is also mirrored in Joseph's speech in Genesis 45. This suggests that Joseph's speech in Genesis 45:1-15 is an important turning point in the larger story. His speech can be outlined in the following manner. The outline will include vv. 16-20 because these verses show the effects of Joseph's speech not only on his family but also on the Egyptians.

I. Joseph identifies himself to his brothers (vv. 1-3)
II. Joseph provides a theological interpretation of his journey into slavery (vv. 4-8)
III. The result of Joseph's theological interpretation (vv. 9-20)
   A. To the family (vv. 9-14)
      1. Father/son (vv. 9-13)
      2. Brothers (vv. 14-15)
   B. To the Egyptians (vv. 16-20)

Signficance. The hiddenness of God that has characterized the Joseph stories up to this point gives way in vv. 5-8, when Joseph identifies himself to his brothers in vv. 1-3, which then provides the context for a theological interpretation of his life's story. Joseph states to his brothers that what they meant for evil, God has meant for good. This interpretation is not really very startling in terms of its theological content, the reader has suspected as much all along. Worth noting, however, is the timing of Joseph's theological insight. God enters the story precisely at the moment when Joseph also undergoes a transformation from being a powerful Egyptian, who is toying with a Canaanite family, to becoming their brother once again. The timing is not a coincidence, for it provides a strong message of how theological insight and proper human action often occur in tandem. The point is not to determine which of the two is prior—human action or theological insight but to realize that revelation and ethical transformation are frequently complementary. Thus whether Joseph's decision to make himself known to his brothers allowed him to see clearly the hand of God in his life's story or whether it was just the reverse—namely that seeing God's hand in his life's story gave Joseph the freedom to become a brother again—does not really matter because the end result is the same: The power of God's promise breaks back into the story, which then pushes the narrative in a new direction toward family unity in vv. 9-15.

Verses 9-15 (16-20) pick up the motifs of family that were central to

Genesis 37. References to son (four times in vv. 9, 10 [three times]) father (six times in vv. 8, 9, 13 [twice], 18, 19) and brother (five times in vv. 12, 14, 15, 16, 17) dominate in the remainder of Joseph's speech, and they are used to create a series of reversals from Genesis 37. Instead of a story where there is no shalom (peace) in the family, which then infiltrates the larger social and political world (from the Ishmaelites and Midianites to the Egyptians), in vv. 9-20 these motifs create family unity (vv. 9-14, father-son; vv. 15-16, brothers or kinship), which then affects the Egyptians in a positive way. Pharaoh is portrayed in vv. 16-20 as welcoming Joseph's family to Egypt and as offering them the best of his country. By the end of this story, we no longer ask where the power of the promise is, because we see that it has infiltrated every corner of Joseph's world.

The preacher, therefore, has opportunity to preach about the hiddenness of God, and the power of dreams in revealing God's will, or the need for seeing God at work through the ordinary events of family life.

The Response: *Psalm 133*

Celebrating Community

Setting. Psalm 133 is categorized as both a wisdom song and a didactic poem. For purposes of worship the difference does not matter. It appears to be a hymn or song of greeting, perhaps used within the context of the wisdom school, but the references to Aaron demonstrate that the song was also taken up into the worship setting, as are many of the Psalms of Ascent (120–134). In this context of worship, Zion is exalted throughout the Psalms of Ascent.

Structure. It is probably best not to break the short psalm into any smaller units. The psalm consists of two similes (oil and dew), which are enveloped by a beatitude about family unity.

Significance. Psalm 133 is undoubtedly chosen to provide commentary on the ending of Genesis 45, where the family is reunited. It puts into liturgical (priestly) language the same theme as the story. The blessing of God makes community possible and is evident in the unity of the community. Both of these statements are true at the same time just as they were in the story of Joseph.

The simile with oil is a priestly reference that creates an analogy between the oil that anoints a priest in the ritual tradition of Aaron and the community that is served by that priest. The simile created with dew is an analogy to the high and holy place on Mount Hermon, where the blessings and peace of God are issued on behalf of Zion, the name for the worshiping community in Israel.

A sermon on this psalm might emphasize the community that is possible when new images of God's blessing are evoked or based on these ancient similes. How is oil used ritually in our day to symbolize the work of the Holy Spirit? How might the morning dew evoke mixed images of God's blessing and simultaneously the evaporation of our efforts (see Hosea 13:3) to be faithful.

New Testament Texts

Strikingly both lessons, though coming through the sequential reading of Romans and Matthew, deal with the the grace of God that extended ultimately and universally to all humanity in Jesus Christ.

The Epistle: *Romans 11:1-2*a, *29-32*

God's Irrevocable Gifts and Calling

Setting. The discussion of setting for Propers 13 and 14 may prove helpful in grasping the context of this week's lesson. Actually these verses from Romans 11 are the conclusion of all of Paul's deliberation through the prose in Romans 9–11. In this lesson Paul articulates the problem that arises through the rejection of the gospel by some Jews, and he comments on the character and purposes of God's work. The concluding verses of Romans 11 (33-36) are a doxology to God based on the "point" Paul makes in the verses of our lesson.

Structure. By taking 11:1-2*a*, 29-32 as the text for this week's reading, the lectionary first sets up the problem Paul debates throughout Romans 9–11 (vv. 1-2*a*), and, then, states Paul's position or conclusion in relation to the matter (vv. 29-32). In the initial verses, one encounters this sequence: (1) rhetorical question, (2) rhetorical answer with illustration, and (3) declaration of truth. In the final verses, we see (1) another declaration of truth, (2) a word of explanation focusing on the human situation, and (3) a word of explanation focusing on God's activity.

Significance. What is one to make of the rejection of the gospel of Jesus Christ by some, even the majority, of God's chosen people—the Jews? Paul wrestles with the problem in Romans 9–11 in an elaborate way, which often leaves us wondering exactly what he said. The whole of the apostle's deliberation, however, is summarized neatly in this lesson. Bluntly stated, the problem is a theological one more so than an anthropological one. Paul does not ask, "Why don't all Jews believe?"; rather, he wonders, "Has God rejected his people?" Notice, Paul assumes that whatever the Jews are doing, or not doing, God is responsible. Paul assumes that God is capable of bringing the chosen people to belief, so that if they do not believe the gospel of Jesus Christ, one must wonder whether God has rejected them, not what is wrong with them.

Paul rejects the conclusion that God has rejected the Jews. His evidence is that he himself, a Jew, believes the gospel. Thus God has brought Paul and some other Jews to faith. One could conclude (and some of Paul's oblique remarks in Romans 9–11 can be read to imply) that God has saved a remnant of the Jews, and that is all God intended to do and that is all God is going to do. But such a conclusion does not fit the evidence of Paul's statements. In Romans 11:2*a*, the apostle boldly declares, "God has not rejected his people whom he foreknew." Exactly what he means by this becomes clear in the final verses of our lesson, when he says, "The gifts and the calling of God are irrevocable." God's choice of the Jews is universal and eternal.

But then, what does it mean that many Jews do not believe. Paul refrains from comment upon Jewish unbelief; rather he explains what is happening in terms of divine activity. And what an odd God we find Paul declaring! John Calvin and others have struggled with the idea of "predestination" (God . . . foreknew), and the image of God constructed in their reflection often seems strange (double-edged predestination!). But from a careful reading of Paul's remarks in Romans 9–11, in fact, the God of Calvin and others is simply not strange enough.

Paul maintains the conviction that God is both sovereign and faithful, so that present Jewish rejection of the gospel is not a sign of

God's rejection of the Jews, but the result of God's working through the Jews, using them, to accomplish the salvation of the Gentiles. Paul's logic is peculiar, but quite clear. God acts freely with the authority of the Creator over creation (including human creatures). Presently God's wrath is upon some while God's mercy rests on others. Yet, the Jewish condition of unbelief is not a permanent state. It is the result of God's using Israel as God's tool in the extension of mercy to all humanity. God hardened part of Israel to save the Gentiles so that ultimately all Israel will be saved. The present situation exists because God is moving toward a goal: to have mercy on all humanity. If God's method seems odd, we should take comfort in Paul's description of God's activity as a mystery.

Perhaps there are three conclusions we may draw in relation to Paul's difficult remarks: (1) God works in ways that elude or baffle the human mind. (2) God is merciful. And, (3) God is faithful. If we grasp Paul's point(s) and if we believe, we may be moved in conclusion, as was the apostle, to the praise of God (11:33-36).

The Gospel: *Matthew 15:(10-20) 21-28*

Great and Unprecedented Faith

Setting. The revision of the lectionary includes the possibility of reading vv. 10-20 with vv. 21-28. The motivation for this expansion of the lesson was to allow vv. 10-20 to provide a setting for the story in vv. 21-28. This well-intended alteration may not, however, prove to be helpful. In fact, vv. 10-20 should be read with vv. 1-9. The particular dispute between Jesus and the Pharisees in vv. 1-9 leads to Jesus' words on the larger issue of ritual purity in vv. 10-20. All of this may provide a backdrop for the story of Jesus and the Canaanite woman, but that story stands easily without the preceding materials. Most likely Matthew is simply following Mark's order, and in Mark there is a clean break between the ritual disputes with the Pharisees and the healing of the Syro-Phoenician woman's daughter, which Matthew preserves by the opening in v. 21, "Jesus left that place and went away to the district of Tyre and Sidon." The comments below deal only with vv. 21-28.

Structure. The story has the normal elements of an ancient miracle account: problem, action/solution, and confirmation. But, it has more! The story gives us the exchange between Jesus and the woman and the note about the disciples' coming and urging Jesus to get rid of the annoying woman. Moreover, the confirmation is neither a demonstration of the health of the one healed nor an awe-inspired reaction from observers. With these alterations in the miracle form, Matthew focuses our attention away from the miracle of healing per se and points us in the direction he would have our minds travel.

Significance. Jesus moves out of his normal locale into the coastal border zone of Tyre and Sidon. A non-Jewish woman (called a Canaanite by Matthew) does an amazing thing, she recognizes Jesus and salutes him with highly honorific titles, "Lord, Son of David." And Jesus himself surprises us. This is the same Jesus who looked with compassion upon the nagging crowds from which he could not escape. This is the Jesus who fed the multitudes. But now he doesn't even bother to answer this woman. The disciples express their own irritation to Jesus and suggest that he do something to relieve them from her shouting. Jesus turns and speaks to the woman, and we learn of his pointed sense of mission to Israel. His statement creates real tension in the narrative. Recall that Jesus has been experiencing rejection and hostility among the people of Israel, but now when he gets the reception he desires from the Canaanite woman, he draws back from any involvement with her that could detract or deter him from the painful service he is in the process of extending to Israel. Yet, the woman's relentless faith wins Jesus over, and we see, apparently along with Jesus in this story, that God's work through Jesus is destined to move beyond the confines of Israel to all persons of faith.

Sermons that take their cue from contemporary sensibilities—and start from the fact that the Canaanite woman is a woman—run at least three risks: (1) they will be necessarily brief, single issue, and done more from the preacher's prejudices than from careful interaction with the text; (2) they will be anthropological rather than theological, and thus not worthy of or dependent upon the Gospel; and (3) they will miss an important message of the text.

In ancient Jewish eyes this Canaanite woman lived with a double liability: she was a woman and she was a Canaanite. The second was far worse than the first, and essentially made the gender issue irrelevant. Her poor daughter had a triple problem: Canaanite, female, and demon-possessed. Jesus identifies the issue in terms of a seemingly impossible distance between the power of God working through him and the needed healing of the Canaanite woman's daughter, because the woman and her daughter were not Israelites. Jesus himself understands the grace of God to be confined, at least for the moment, to the children of Israel.

What we witness in this story is the grace of God finding its way beyond the religious and national lines of ethnic Israel. We have here a glimpse of the future of the gospel, where the power of God will be extended to all people of faith. The story tells us dramatically that the time for universal grace is now. Too often we live as if we are waiting to be given permission or directions to extend God's grace to all persons in all places, but in fact we read this lesson and we see that God's grace is naturally and always for all people. The text should drive us past our prejudices, and it should direct us to missions. There are strong ethical and profound evangelical dimensions to this passage, both of which should be treated in proclamation.

Proper 15: The Celebration

Today's epistle may serve as a hermeneutical tool for discussing either the Old Testament lesson or the Gospel (short form). The providence of God is the major theme for Paul as he discusses how both Jew and Gentile will be brought to the fullness of salvation. The providence of God is the issue in Genesis when Joseph declares to his brothers that though they meant him harm, God intended it for good. And in the Gospel we see the beginning of the process by which the good news will be proclaimed to the Gentiles. This set of lessons provides a fine example of how, even when pericopes are being chosen sequentially with no necessary intent for thematic harmonization, the great themes of Scripture will make themselves evident and challenge the preacher to enter into dialogue with them.

The worship leader is encouraged to extend the epistle through vv. 33-36. This is a great doxology in praise of God's providence, a fitting end to two lessons that deal with the accomplishment of reconciliation. If those verses are not used as part of the epistle reading, they may be used as a congregational response to the reading either in prose or in the following stanza from John Henry Newman:

Praise to the Holiest in the height,
  And in the depth be praise;
In all his words most wonderful,
  Most sure in all his ways.

Certain hymns relating to the providence of God should be considered when planning for this service.

All my hope is firmly grounded
Children of the heavenly Father
God moves in a mysterious way
  (O God, in a mysterious way)
God of our life, through all the circling years
If thou but suffer God to guide thee
We gather together to ask the Lord's blessing.

The Presbyterian Hymnal contains an inclusive language metrical version of Psalm 133.

If the Eucharist is celebrated on this day, "God of Our Life, Through All the Circling Years" would be an appropriate offertory hymn with its concluding line, "Be thou for us in life our daily bread." Today's Gospel is the source for the image, "gather up the crumbs under thy table," in Cranmer's Prayer of Humble Access. Although that prayer has been omitted from many revised liturgies, it would be appropriate as a prayer of preparation printed for private use at the beginning of the bulletin or as a unison conclusion to the Prayers of the People. Following are two versions of it as now employed in the Church of England, in its *Alternative Service Book 1980*.

(1) We do not presume
to come to this your table, merciful Lord,
trusting in our own righteousness,
but in your manifold and great mercies.
We are not worthy
so much as to gather up the crumbs under your table.
But you are the same Lord
whose nature is always to have mercy.
Grant us therefore, gracious Lord,
so to eat the flesh of your dear son Jesus Christ
and to drink his blood,
that we may evermore dwell in him
and he in us. Amen.

(2) Most merciful Lord,
your love compels us to come in.
Our hands were unclean,
our hearts were unprepared;
we were not fit
even to eat the crumbs from under your table.
But you, Lord, are the God of our salvation,
and share your bread with sinners.
So cleanse and feed us
with the precious body and blood of your Son,
that he may live in us and we in him;
may sit and eat in your kingdom. Amen.

Proper Sixteen
Sunday Between August 21 and 27 Inclusive

Old Testament Texts

Exodus 1:8–2:10 contains three stories that explore the power of salvation, while Psalm 124 turns the insights gained from the introductory stories in Exodus into the language of praise.

The Lesson: *Exodus 1:8–2:10*

The Salvation of the Savior

Setting. Moses is the central human character in the book of Exodus and, indeed, in the remainder of the Pentateuch. He is the one called by God to be the savior. With this knowledge as background, it is easy to conclude that the central event in the Old Testament lesson for this Sunday is the account of his birth in Exodus 2:1-10, and the present interpretation has followed this insight as a starting point. Yet, as soon as the central role of Moses is established, the opening stories to the book of Exodus present a new set of problems because of the way in which Moses is introduced. He enters the story as a vulnerable infant, who is born with a death threat hanging over his head from the most powerful person in the world, Pharaoh. In the light of this near hopeless situation an unlikely cast of characters—two midwives, a slave mother and her daughter, and eventually even Pharaoh's own daughter—team up to save the future savior. This pitting of the women against Pharaoh provides the setting for the biblical writers to explore different kinds of power in this world. Their aim is to provide us with guidelines for evaluating which kinds of power come from God.

Structure. The earlier conclusion that Exodus 1:8–2:10 is primarily about the birth of Moses is somewhat misleading, because the birth of Moses is really the last of three stories that explore power from a number of different perspectives: how we as humans abuse power, how God uses power in spite of us, and how this situation creates conflict in our world. The three stories in Exodus 1:8–2:10 are: vv. 8-14, the account of Israel's forced labor; vv. 15-21, the first account of male genocide when only the midwives are commanded to kill Israelite babies; and, 1:22–2:10, the second account of male genocide when all Egyptians are commanded to kill Israelite babies. The birth of Moses takes place in the last story. These three stories can be outlined into two sections under the headings of forced labor and male genocide.

I. Pharaoh's Command for Forced Labor and the Continued Multiplication of the Israelites (vv. 8-14)
   A. The threat of Israel's increasing numbers (vv. 8-10)
   B. The raising up of taskmasters (vv. 11-14)
II. Pharaoh's Command for Male Genocide and the Salvation of the Savior (1:15–2:10)
   A. The story of the midwives (vv. 7-21)
   B. The story of the Levite mother, her daughter, and the daughter of Pharaoh

Significance. The conflict between Pharaoh and Israel/midwives/a Levitical mother is a clash of two kinds of power. Pharaoh represents the pinnacle of human power. He is someone who controls worlds and the fate of entire groups of people. Israel, the midwives, and the Levitical mother represent the power of God's promise. These characters do not control worlds; in fact, they do not even control their own destinies. The surprising twist in the opening chapters of Exodus is that these seemingly powerless characters are the ones who create dread in Pharaoh, while Pharaoh's imperial commands have little or no effect on them. This situation gives the powerful Pharaoh an almost buffoonish aura in the opening chapters of Exodus as he bumbles along from failure to failure. Juxtaposed to him are the women, who model what the power of salvation is like, and thus how saviors must act in this world. The end result of their action is that they save the future savior, Moses, from Pharaoh. A brief overview of the three stories will illustrate the important role of the women as those who model the power of salvation.

First, the story of forced labor in vv. 8-14. Verse 8 informs the reader that a new pharaoh now rules, who does not share the attitude of the pharaoh who raised up Joseph and willingly gave the best of Egyptian land and produce to Israel. Although this new pharaoh initiates all action in the opening chapters, his first words in v. 8 provide clear indication that with all his power he is not the one in control. His opening speech gives insight to a sense of dread. He states that the Israelites are now "too many and too mighty" for the Egyptians. He has good reason to fear because Israel has the power of the divine blessing; and, as we saw in earlier lessons from Genesis, one of the effects of this is that they cannot help reproducing. Thus they are growing in number and Pharaoh is insecure. His solution is to use his power oppressively. Yet v. 12 illustrates the subversive power of the blessing, for the reader is told that the more Pharaoh oppressed Israel the more quickly they reproduced and spread around Egypt. The picture reminds one of a colony of rabbits.

Second, the story of the midwives in vv. 15-21. Pharaoh moves to more desperate measures in vv. 15-16 by commanding two midwives, Shiphrah and Puah, to kill all Israelite male children. This holocaust is thwarted because the midwives feared God (v. 17), didn't follow the orders of Pharaoh (v. 17), and then lied about it (vv. 18-19). The result of the heroic action of the midwives is that the power of the divine blessing now begins to influence their families, while it also continues to produce more and more Israelites.

Third, the birth story of Moses in 1:22–2:10. The birth story of Moses is really the second episode in Pharaoh's attempt to stop the growth of Israel through genocide. In v. 22 all Egyptians are commanded to kill all Hebrew male babies by drowning them in the Nile. The command is no sooner out of the mouth of Pharaoh before it clashes again with the power of God's blessing, for the reader is told in 2:1 that a Levitical woman became pregnant and gave birth to a son. This is the third clash between the fear of Pharaoh and the power of

God's blessing; and, even though this episode introduces the heroic child Moses, the reader is now able to predict the outcome. This child is not going to die. What is surprising is how the power of God's blessing even begins to infiltrate Pharaoh's own household, through the back door so to speak, when Moses is saved by Pharaoh's own daughter.

Exodus 1:8–2:10 tells the same story three times. It is a story of how the power of God's blessing cannot be stopped by any human power, and this certainly provides a central point for preaching. Furthermore, in the telling of the story, biblical writers have provided a model of what human power should be like if we believe in the power of God's blessing, and this model is not risk free. The midwives and the Levitical woman defied the political powers in their quest to preserve life. In so doing they are the first saviors in the book of Exodus, and they provide the model by which all future saviors, including Moses, will be judged.

The Response: *Psalm 124*

Learning the Language of Praise

Setting. Psalm 124 is frequently classified as a song of thanksgiving. The thanks that is directed to God in vv. 6-7 provides a strong basis for such a conclusion. Recently, scholars have argued that the psalm also has an instructional side to it, especially in vv. 1-5, where a threatening situation is described without any divine intervention. Psalm 124, therefore, must be seen as providing both instruction on how God acts in events and language of thanksgiving.

Structure. Psalm 124 separates into three parts.

I. Instruction (vv. 1-5)
II. Thanksgiving (vv. 6-7)
III. Concluding Confession (v. 8)

Significance. The language of the psalm provides direct commentary on the opening chapters of Exodus. The center of the psalm is vv. 6-7 where God is momentarily praised for having saved Israel from an overpowering enemy. The language of praise in vv. 6-7 takes on significance because of the hypothetical scenario that is sketched out in vv. 1-5 of what might have happened without God's help. The psalm ends in v. 8 with a confession that, indeed, Israel's help is rooted in God alone.

New Testament Texts

Both lessons treat practical matters of daily Christian life, though in very different ways. Despite the distinctions in forms, however, the understanding of Christian faith and practice in the texts is highly compatible.

The Epistle: *Romans 12:1-8*

Present Your Bodies to God

Setting. Having grappled with the current relationship between God and the disbelieving portion of Israel and having finally declared his confidence and praise for the irresistible mercy of God (11:32-36), Paul turns in a new direction at Romans 12:1. In the passages that follow Paul is concerned with relating the will of God to the everyday life of the Christian community. He begins somewhat abstractly, but along the way he becomes steadily more specific through the end of the letter.

Structure. Our lesson falls into two recognizable but related parts: vv. 1-2 and vv. 3-8. It is possible to understand the second part of the lesson as an elaboration of the statements made in vv. 1-2. Paul makes an appeal (vv. 1 and 3), which he bases on the sympathetic purposes of God (vv. 1 and 3), for the Roman Christians to give themselves without reservation to execution of God's will (vv. 1-2 and 4-8). In v. 2 Paul also sounds a note, calling the Romans away from involvement with the present age (literally "this age" in Greek, not "this world" as in NRSV), which he comes back to only in vv. 9-21.

Significance. Paul's language betrays a sense of earnest urgency at the outset of this passage. The Greek word translated "I appeal" is the normal language of a trial lawyer urging a jury to the verdict that is advocated by the attorney. Thus Paul's vocabulary itself informs us of the tone and dynamics of this passage, and the sermon will do well to follow Paul's lead. Paul trusts the Romans to reason along with him to a common conclusion, so that he is neither teaching them a lesson nor giving them a pep-talk. He is persuading vigorously.

The foundation of Paul's appeal is the very "mercies" of God. God has fully sympathized with the human situation, and this has profound implications for the way that Christians are now to go about life. Because of God's full sympathy with the human condition, those who by grace have been called to faith in Christ can give themselves in full confidence to God's purposes. Presenting our bodies may, however, strike us as a peculiar form of "spiritual worship." When it comes to spirituality, we usually experience a hankering for lofty thoughts, lovely feelings, and unseen things. But the word Paul uses, which many translations render "spiritual," is in fact a nearly technical term meaning "uniquely human" in relation to "that which is logical." And so the KJV translated "reasonable worship." Indeed, Paul is telling us something here, though he is not primarily giving us a lesson; Paul works from the assumption that Christian faith is a reasonable and real life of practical service to God. Our faith is not essentially the pursuit of mystical dreams and sensational emotions. Believers in a Christ who himself died on a cross in faithful obedience to God's will cannot expect anything other than a kind of worship that calls for the very real giving of their physical selves to the doing of God's work.

The call to physical service as an expression of our gratitude to and adoration of God may run counter to the normal religious expectations of our times. Frankly, in our world people generally practice Christian faith for the benefits that are derived from it; so it shouldn't surprise us that part of Paul's appeal is that the Romans live differently from the ways of the world. Our faith is not for service to selfishness; it is a call to selflessness, to Christlikeness.

While the call to common service unites us as believers, Paul continues by stating that the service to which we each are called will be different. God has granted us a host of complementary gifts and skills, and we are to assess our talents realistically and ask what it is that God would have us do. Paul lists several possibilities in vv. 6-8, but his remarks are more illustrations than an exhaustive catalogue of graces. What finally determines whether a particular capacity is apt for Christian service is whether we are serving Christ and Christ's body or ourselves. For example, a beautiful voice can be employed for praising God or edifying the worship life of a congregation, or it can, even in the context of religious devotion, be a vehicle for simple self-aggrandizement.

The Gospel: *Matthew 16:13-20*

Faith That Brings Authority

Setting. In discussing the setting for last Sunday's Gospel lesson, we noticed the actual distance between the story of the healing of the Canaanite woman's daughter and the previous verses, which told of some of the controversies Jesus engaged in with the Pharisees. After a series of stories (Matthew 15:29-39), Matthew returned in his account of Jesus' ministry to tell of still further give-and-take between Jesus and the Jewish authorities (16:1-4), and then again, Matthew reports Jesus' negative judgment of the leaders (16:5-12). Our lesson follows these passages, and it is distinct from them, although it is set among them. In 16:13-20 Jesus turns away from the Jewish authorities to his disciples.

Structure. There are two parts to the lesson: vv. 13-16 and 20, which are comparable with Mark 8:27-30 and Luke 9:18-21; and vv. 17-19, which are without parallel in the other Gospels. The manner in which Matthew splices vv. 17-19 into the material in vv. 13-16 and 20 indicates his understanding of the interrelatedness of the two parts of the lesson.

Significance. The passage relates Christian faith and basic authority for ministry in a crucial fashion. The manner in which Matthew recounts the famous confession of Peter at Caesarea Philippi communicates a number of convictions about the nature of valid faith. First, faith is informed. Jesus assumes that his disciples are aware of what people are saying about him. They are not isolated and ignorant of the options for comprehending the person and work of Jesus. Second, faith is involved. It is not enough merely to mouth the opinions of others. We must grapple with the issues of faith ourselves and form a conviction that is genuinely ours. Third, faith is independent. We may be called to draw conclusions that differ from those currently available through traditional channels. We are called to fresh assessment of Jesus Christ that makes our faith vital, real, and capable of robust declaration. Fourth, faith is inspired. What we know about the person, work, and will of our Lord Jesus Christ is not so much the result of our own musings as it is the outcome of the work of God in our lives. These four characteristics or dimensions of faith are the basis of the words of Jesus to Simon Peter, "Blessed are you, Simon son of Jonah!" As we manifest the kind of faith expressed by Peter, we too can count on hearing the blessing of our Lord.

Yet, Matthew structures this passage in such a way as to show us that faith is not merely static, not merely something we have that brings us a divine blessing. Having recognized the validity of Simon Peter's faith, Jesus spoke further about the responsibilities inherent in a dynamic faith. Jesus gives the faith-filled Peter the charge to and authority for doing the work of God on this earth. Peter is not turned into a little God, but his faith means that he is charged with the power of God for doing God's will. There are at least two dimensions to the work to which Peter is directed. First, he is to give himself to the service of the Church. Christ's charge to ministry calls Peter to bear the weight of the Church, providing through the strength of God-given faith the support the Church needs to be established in the world. Second, Peter is directed beyond the walls of the Church to work "on earth." This kind of ministry is the establishment of God's ways among humanity. Whether we call it social action or community service, Jesus' words hold the germ of the idea of the people of faith being concerned with more than the community of faith.

Finally, in Jesus' words to Simon Peter we see a word of warning about the difficulties we can expect to face in ministry. "The gates of Hades" will rail against those in service through faith. But Jesus' words also contain an assurance that we will be sustained in our faithful efforts, "the gates of Hades will not prevail." Thus the gift of authority for ministry is not a call to privilege, position, and power; rather, it is a directive to the hard work of ministry wherein we can count on opposition, but wherein we are guaranteed divine support. Faith inspired by God empowers us for service and grants us the confidence that the God who inspired and directed us to service is with us in ministry, regardless of all difficulties.

Proper 16: The Celebration

Just as the commentator on today's epistle warns us against a vapid understanding of "spiritual," far removed from what Paul intended, so the preacher should also beware individualistic and privatistic interpretations of today's lections, lest we do violence to their communal character. The Old Testament lesson is not simply about the birth of a hero of mythic proportions; it is a continuation of that narrative of the promise to Abraham that he would be the father of many nations. The ministry of Moses can only be understood in the light of the demand to "let my people go." Paul's ethical exhortations are aimed at the community that he has been addressing. He stresses their incorporation into that same covenant relationship that began with Abraham and was sustained through Moses, and which must express itself in terms of the use of gifts given in the service of one another. Peter's declaration is affirmed by Jesus in relationship to the Church, to the assembly of believers, and not as a private pat on the back for Peter, who answered right when questioned. The preacher should struggle, then, to balance the individual and corporate aspects of the texts and not use them as lists or anagrams for effective living. There is an ecclesiological issue to be dealt with in each text, so the preacher might have some success by beginning to meditate on the question, "What has this text to say about what it means to be a part of the Church, of the body of Christ?"

The following Doddridge hymn can serve effectively as a bridge between the epistle and the Gospel, since it reflects elements of both. It understands the corporate nature of the Church to be that which spans time as well as space and takes seriously the difference in function given to members of the body. The tune Duke Street fits it well.

The Savior, when to heaven he rose,
In splendid triumph o'er his foes,
Scattered his gifts on us below,
And wide his royal bounties flow.

Hence sprung the apostles' honored name,
Sacred beyond heroic fame;
In lowlier forms, to bless our eyes,
Pastors from hence, and teachers rise.

From Christ their varied gifts derive,
And, fed by Christ, their graces live;
While, guarded by his mighty hand,
Midst all the rage of hell they stand.

So shall the bright succession run
Through the last courses of the sun;
While unborn churches by their care
Shall rise and flourish large and fair.

Jesus our Lord their hearts shall know—
The Spring whence all these blessings flow;
Pastors and people shout his praise
Through all the round of endless days.

Hymns of a more individualistic flavor for this day might include "Onward, Christian Soldiers," "Forth in Thy Name," and "Take My Life, and Let It Be."

The following collect from *Lesser Feasts and Fasts* may serve as the day's opening prayer or as part of the petitions:

> Almighty Father, who inspired Simon Peter, first among the apostles, to confess Jesus as Messiah and Son of the living God: Keep your Church steadfast upon the rock of this faith, so that in unity and peace we may proclaim the one truth and follow the one Lord, our Savior Jesus Christ; who lives and reigns with you and the Holy Spirit, one God, now and for ever. (Copyright © 1988 The Church Pension Fund. Used by Permission.)

Proper Seventeen Sunday Between August 28 and September 3 Inclusive

Old Testament Texts

Exodus 3:1-15 is the call of Moses, which ends with the revelation of the divine name, while Psalm 105:1-6, 23-26, 45*b* adds an alternative section (vv. 23-26) to the historical hymn of praise that was also the psalm for Proper Fourteen. The replacement section recounts Israel's oppression in Egypt and the calling of Moses and Aaron to save them.

The Lesson: *Exodus 3:1-15*

Deciphering God's Call

Setting. Exodus 3:1-15 is best characterized as a call narrative. The call narrative is an established genre that biblical writers frequently use to tell the story of how a person was called by God. Call narratives are primarily associated with prophetic heroes like Isaiah (Isaiah 6) or Jeremiah (Jeremiah 1), but they are also used in narrative settings to explore how heroes like Moses or Gideon (Judges 6) were confronted by God with a task. The call narrative is a powerful form of speech because it tends to follow a typical sequence of action and dialogue, so that the ancient listener had expectations that aided interpretation of the story.

Structure. Call narratives have been studied extensively and tend to follow, according to Norman Habel (*Zeitschrift fur die altestamentliche Wissenschaft*, 1965), a six-part sequence of action that consists of divine confrontation, introductory word, omission, objection, reassurance, and sign. The call of Moses in Exodus 3:1-15 can be outlined under these six headings in the following manner.

I. Introductory word (vv. 1-3)
  A. Moses is in the midst of his daily routine
  B. God appears to him in a burning bush unexpectedly and disrupts his routine
II. Introductory word (vv. 4-9)
  A. The introductory word is a divine speech that arouses the attention of Moses
  B. The speech delineates a relationship between God, Moses, and the people of God
  C. The relationship will provide the basis for a commission to Moses
III. Commission—bring Israel from Egypt (v. 10)
IV. Objection—Who am I? (v. 11)
V. Reassurance—I will be with you (v. 12*a*)
VI. Sign (vv. 12*b*-15)
  A. Israel will worship God in the mountain (v. 12*b*)
  B. YHWH: the divine name (vv. 13-15)

Significance. The structure of the call form carries a message about who God is and how we go about deciphering the call of God in our lives. Thus by applying the call form to Moses in Exodus 3:1-15, biblical writers were not simply trying to show that Moses was authentically called by God, they are also inviting the readers to apply the call form to their own lives. What is a call from God? And how can we extract a theology from the call form that can be the basis for a contemporary proclamation? An answer to this question will be the goal of the remainder of our analysis of Exodus 3:1-15.

The call form suggests several important things about how we go about looking for the call of God.

First, the divine confrontation encourages us to look for the call of God in the ordinary experience of our everyday routines. Moses is tending sheep, he is not out looking for a mountaintop experience. Frequently the call of God to biblical characters is unexpected. This stereotyped aspect of call narratives suggests that we should not be looking for the call of God as something special or as something in addition to our routine, but as something that arises from it.

Second, the introductory word tends to establish a relationship between God and the one being called, which gives a new perspective on life that enables someone to have a call. In the case of Moses, God had to recount the entire history of salvation to provide a new perspective for Israel's future savior. In fact, one could argue that in Exodus 3 Moses does not even know who God is, much less who his ancestors were, since he is introduced to us as an adopted Egyptian who has now fled to Midian and married into a priestly family.

Third, the commission from God is always very specific and task oriented. Biblical characters are neither called to have a particular state of mind or attitude toward the world nor to abstract ideas. Rather, the divine call in Scripture always arises out of specific situations that require a concrete task. For Moses, the task is to lead Israel out of Egypt.

Fourth, it is essential to see that objection to the divine call is orthodox. If one does not feel a sense of objection at some point to the call, perhaps it is not the call of God. Or perhaps our human ambitions have crowded out the call. Moses immediately tells God that he cannot lead Israel from Egypt. Biblical writers are telling us at least two things by incorporating an objection into the standard form of call narratives: that as humans we are inherently inadequate to fulfill any divine call and that there is risk in being called by God, which we would rather avoid upon first instinct.

Fifth, objection always prompts divine reassurance. God's response to Moses in v. 12*a* ("I will be with you") is more or less the standard divine reassurance that is given throughout the call narratives. This reassurance requires a second look from us because it is neither a guarantee of success nor a psychological pat on the back. God does not respond to Moses by telling him that he has innate qualities of leadership that simply must be brought out. Rather, the reassurance is a divine commitment to share the risk of the one being called. Thus following a call from God means that we will never be alone, even though we may fail. Different biblical characters achieve different levels of success in following the divine call. Moses is partially successful, since he does, indeed, lead Israel out of Egypt. However, he does not bring them into the land of Canaan. Other characters like Jeremiah are even less successful in achieving change by following their commissions. It is important to see that biblical characters are not evaluated by their successes but by their courage (faith) in following their commission.

Sixth, call narratives often end with a sign. Thus after biblical characters go through the drama of having their routine disrupted by God, receiving a commission, and then objecting to it, they still are required to test the call further, by asking for a sign. In other words, characters do not act impulsively. In the call of Moses God must first introduce the element of a sign in v. 12*a*. This fits the character of Moses, because he is presented to us in Exodus 3 as someone who does not really know who God is. Thus the introductory word in vv. 4-9 was nothing less than God's entire resume of salvation. Once God introduces the aspect of a sign in the call process, Moses doesn't hesitate to use it, for the rest of Exodus 3 and much of Exodus 4 is a sequence of stories in which Moses tests God and asks for different signs until he finally starts for Egypt in Exodus 4:18.

To summarize: Call narratives have at least two functions in biblical literature, which must be kept in mind when preaching Exodus 3. First, they authenticate certain characters for us. When viewed from this perspective, biblical writers are telling the reader that the actions of a hero must be read in the light of a larger story about God's salvation. Second, biblical call narratives are also meant to provide a structure whereby the people of God in any age can evaluate God's call. This aspect of call narratives makes them a powerful channel for proclamation, for we, the hearers of the text, are invited to use this structure for evaluating God's call in our lives.

The Response: *Psalm 105:1-6, 23-26, 45*b

A Song of Praise

Setting. Psalm 105:1-6, 23-26, 45*b*, the account of Joseph being sold into slavery, was the psalm reading for Proper Fourteen. See that entry for introductory commentary on this psalm.

Structure. The lectionary reading includes the introductory call to give thanks in vv. 1-6, the account of Israelite oppression in Egypt in vv. 23-25, the sending of Moses and Aaron in v. 26, and the benediction of praise for God's statutes in 45*b*.

Significance. Psalm 105:1-6, 23-26, 45*b* takes up the narrative account of Israel in Egypt and turns it into the language of praise. Note how all the events in Egypt are redefined with God as their subject: the Lord made his people fruitful and strong, the Lord turns the Egyptians against Israel, and then the Lord sent Moses and Aaron. This text is not a theodicy, but it is a confessional response to suffering in the context of worship. The point is the same as the reassurance in the call narrative, namely that God is present with Israel, sharing their risk at a time of oppression, and that God is also their Savior.

New Testament Texts

The text from Romans advocates a genuinely Christian life-style based on full confidence in God; and the Gospel reading focuses on two related passages concerned with the character of Christ's ministry and the character of discipleship.

The Epistle: *Romans 12:9-21*

Trusting God and Living a Life of Genuine Love

Setting. The discussion of the setting of last week's lesson is applicable to the lesson for this Sunday, so readers are asked to return to that material. Furthermore, in considering the structure of the preceding verses, Romans 12:1-8, we saw how Paul's essential thought in 12:1-2 is reiterated and amplified in vv. 3-8. We also noticed how Paul's directive in 12:2, "Do not be conformed to this world [literally "this age" in Greek], but be transformed by the renewing of your minds, so that you may discern what is the will of God—what is good and acceptable and perfect," is partially put on hold for more elaborate reflection in vv. 9-21.

Structure. Translations often divide these verses into two paragraphs, vv. 9-13 and vv. 15-21. But in fact the passage is one grand elliptical thought. A reader can take this passage and begin anywhere and continue reading through the ending to the beginning and back around to the starting point. Try it; start at any verse and read around the text. Indeed though there are plenty of pointed remarks between v. 9 and v. 21, these two verses together summarize (a bit abstractly) everything Paul says in the other verses.

Significance. While in the previous lines of Romans 12 Paul was forming an appeal and not engaging in teaching, in these verses he takes out his lecture notes and gives the Romans a lesson. He announces his topic in v. 9: Live a life of genuine love. But while love is the theme, we do not encounter a unified, developing discussion of love such as that found in I Corinthians 13. Here, the apostle is much more practical and far less poetic. The lines of advice assembled here have the appearance of catechistic materials, so that Paul may be going over familiar teachings with the Romans. The statements are generally self-evident, and only two points need highlighting or clarification.

First, the closest Paul comes in these verses to mounting a sustained, coherent argument is in vv. 17-21. At the heart of Paul's remarks is the strong conviction that God is the final authority in human relations. Recognizing that God has the final say in judging the appropriateness of human actions sets one free to live graciously toward others. The security that comes from knowing that God distinguishes right from wrong and promises judgment allows the Christians to get past the need to get even. The basis for peace, love, and harmony is sheerly theological. Whenever we reduce our dealings with others to a merely anthropological level, we are in peril of lapsing into arrogance, indifference, and spitefulness. But, secure in the knowledge of God's concern with and involvement in human affairs, we are free to act kindly and generously toward others.

Second, v. 20 can be misunderstood to refer to a kind of perverse retribution where seeming acts of mercy are in fact masked means of revenge. But v. 21 makes this interpretation impossible. Commentators regularly clarify this difficult idea ("heaping burning coals on their heads") by referring to an ancient Egyptian rite of penitence in which a container of burning coals was carried about on the head to symbolize the repentance of a changed and purified mind. Thus Paul is saying that expressions of genuine love toward enemies will move them to repentance. Given the theological cast of Paul's remarks through this whole text, this is likely more than a wish, a hope, or a pleasant thought. Paul is probably persuaded of the veracity of this advice because he lives with the strong conviction that God is thoroughly involved in human affairs. When things are left to God things turn out well. That is not to say humans are passive, rather they are free to live lives of genuine love because they trust God.

The Gospel: *Matthew 16:21-28*

Hard Sayings on Lordship and Discipleship

Setting. The Gospel lesson for this week follows on the heels of the text for last Sunday, so readers should turn to the discussion of setting for the Gospel text for Proper Sixteen.

Structure. The passage falls into two broad sections, vv. 21-23 and vv. 24-28. Each of these sections has identifiable parts. First, in v. 21 we have the report of Jesus' initial prediction of his forthcoming suffering, death, and Resurrection; and, then, vv. 22-23 tell of a sharp exchange between Peter and Jesus wherein Jesus has the final word. Second, in vv. 24-28 we see a series of five sequential statements by Jesus. Initially, v. 24 declares a standard. Then, in vv. 25, 26, and 27 there are three statements that build off the declaration in v. 24, because each opens with the causal conjunction "for," which introduces an explanation. Finally, v. 28 completes the series of statements by making a further declaration that seems to function as an enigmatic promise.

Significance. The nature of the ministry of Jesus and the nature of the discipleship to which Jesus calls us are hard to comprehend. So when Jesus spoke to his disciples about his destiny—to suffer, to die, and to be raised—we should not be surprised to find Simon Peter trying to set his master straight. After all, Jesus had just told Peter that he had been blessed with the divinely revealed truth that Jesus was the Christ, the Son of the living God; and in affirmation of Peter's faith Jesus had promised him the authority to do the hard work of ministry. This well-informed and authorized disciple heard his master—the

Christ, the Son of the living God—talking about his Passion, and Jesus' words completely threw him. Peter acted quite logically: he rebuked Jesus. Whatever he said, Peter's words were strong; for the verb translated "to rebuke" is the same word used throughout the Gospel in reference to Jesus' rebuking demons. Yet it is Jesus, not Peter, who had the final say in this matter; and his own words, given to us by Matthew, are sharp, "Get behind me, Satan! You are a stumbling block to me; for you are setting your mind not on divine things but on human things." Four items leap to our attention. First, Jesus calls Peter "Satan." As Satan had tempted Jesus in the wilderness, now Peter tempts Jesus by attempting to turn him away from the hard road ahead. Second, Jesus orders Peter, "Get behind me." This is not a dismissal, "Get lost!" but a call to Peter to assume his proper place as a disciple. The same words in Greek formed the call of Peter and Andrew in Matthew 4:19. Third, Jesus tells Peter he is a stumbling block, because Peter's call away from the cross sets before Jesus the scandalous possibility of not suffering, dying, and being raised—the very acts that Jesus says will bring salvation for humanity (see 20:28). Strikingly, the possibility of disobedience to God's will seems real for Jesus, but he rejects this temptation. Fourth, having called Peter "Satan," having called him back into line, and having refused the scandalous option of disobedience, Jesus tells Peter that his mind is set on human things, not the divine. Jesus lived obediently and he served selflessly; but, in contrast, Peter seems to think only of the easy road and the good times. Peter, though recognizing Jesus, still does not comprehend the call to discipleship as a call to service, rather he frames it as a call to privilege and power. And Jesus labels such thinking as typically human and not divine.

In the lines that follow Jesus teaches about the nature of true discipleship. The call to discipleship is a call to become like our Lord, selfless and obedient. The tragic truth is that selfishness, self-centeredness, and self-seeking cut us off from the experience of genuine life, whereas giving ourselves in full service to Christ brings us into true life. Freedom is founded by God in selflessness and obedience (or service).

Along with these lessons about discipleship, Matthew reports two further statements from Jesus. Verse 27 is still another explanation for why disciples should or must live like their Lord. But now, rather than reasoning about life, this statement issues a combined promise and threat. Judgment day is coming, and people will be repaid for what they have done. This is not an admonition to a life of works-righteousness, but it is a frank recognition that what we say and do and how we live make a difference. God has standards, and our lives will be summarized in relation to God's ways. For those undertaking true discipleship to Jesus Christ, this statement is more a word of comfort than a threat. The final declaration (v. 28) also seems to be a promise, though interpreters have long struggled to comprehend the exact meaning of this statement. On the surface it appears that Jesus uttered a false prophecy, for all those standing there died and this world goes on still waiting for "the Son of Man coming in his kingdom." Among the many explanations offered for v. 28, perhaps the most sensible is one that understands this remark in the over-all context of Matthew's Gospel, so that the promise of "the Son of Man coming in his kingdom" is related to the Resurrection appearances of Jesus, especially to the last scene of the Gospel where Jesus says, "All authority in heaven and on earth has been given to me."

Proper 17: The Celebration

The Old Testament's emphasis today on God as I AM leads naturally to the use of "The God of Abraham Praise" as an opening hymn. The Gospel obviously calls for something like "Must Jesus Bear the Cross Alone" or " 'Take Up Thy Cross,' the Savior Said."

The emphasis on call in the Old Testament and on bearing one's cross in the New Testament can be used together in exploring what it means to hear and answer God's call.

Where it is not used as a reading, the epistle may provide a model for the day's prayer of confession if it be used as a kind of checklist for examination of conscience. Or the prayer of confession might follow the epistle reading after a time of silent recollection. Worship planners might consider that prayers of confession are to be followed by some form of absolution or words of assurance and pardon. Verses 11 and 12 from the epistle might also be used for the dismissal at the conclusion of the service; v. 13 can serve as today's offertory sentence. Here is how a premier preacher, writing one hundred years ago, related today's Old Testament lesson to his hearers:

> What thrilled [Moses], and what after all these centuries thrills us, is the personal cry, ''Moses, Moses!'' This offer of personal intimacy between God and man is the heart of Jewish and Christian faith; the ringing, imperative, thrilling voice that cries, Abraham! Moses! Samuel! David! Saul! The faith of the world has been kept alive by the men who have this vivid and unwavering sense of the Divine urgency. Not by the saints of the Bible only, or the saints of the calendar. There are others also, renowned and unrenowned—Bernard and Bunyan and Blandina and Florence Nightingale and Luther and Pascal and Edwards and Wesley and Fliedner, and a glorious company whose names are known to the recording angel only. These have known that they believed in God and have looked for His appearing; but they have known a thing more glorious, that God believed in them, believed in them in spite of defects and narrowness. The strength of such a vision lies just there; not merely in God's appearing, but in His trusting one with a task, in His singling one out for some fine enterprise. We imagine that we must be always finding God; salvation comes with the discovery that God is seeking us. The majesty of Him, the vastness of His dominion, the sweep of His intelligence, the eternity of His being,—these are overwhelming. There is awful meaning in the words, *No man can see My face and live.* But when in some unexpected hour, after a fierce temptation or a bitter disappointment or a frustrated undertaking or a long and weary waiting, the still small Voice calls one by name as He called Moses, and offers one an opportunity or illuminates a duty, then one knows that the Redeemer liveth. Then one knows that one's way is not hid from the Lord in the multitude of His doings. (Charles J. Little, *The Angel in the Flame* [Cincinnati: Jennings and Pye, 1904], pp. 21-23)

SCRIPTURE INDEX

Scripture Index

Old Testament

New Testament

A COMPARISON OF MAJOR LECTIONARIES

A Comparison of Major Lectionaries

YEAR A: TIME AFTER PENTECOST (TRINITY AND PROPERS 6-17)

	Old Testament	Psalm	Epistle	Gospel
		TRINITY SUNDAY		
RCL	Gen. 1:1–2:4*a*	8	II Cor. 13:11-13	Matt. 28:16-20
RoCath	Exod. 34:4-6, 8-9	29–34	II Cor. 13:11-13	John 3:16-18
Episcopal	Gen. 1:1–2:3	150	II Cor. 13:(5-10)11-14	
Lutheran	Gen. 1:1–2:3	29	II Cor. 13:11-14	
		PROPER 6 [RoCath: 11th Ordinary Time] [Luth: 4th After Pentecost]		
RCL	Gen. 18:1-15, (21:1-7)	116:1-2, 12-19	Rom. 5:6-11	Matt. 9:35–10:8 (9-23)
RoCath	Exod. 19:2-6	100:1-3, 5		Matt. 9:35–10:8
Episcopal	Exod. 19:2-8*a*	100		Matt. 9:35–10:8 (9-15)
Lutheran	Exod. 19:2-8*a*	100		Matt. 9:35–10:8

	Old Testament	Psalm	Epistle	Gospel
		PROPER 7 (June 19-25) [RoCath: 12th Ordinary Time] [Luth: 5th After Pentecost]		
RCL	Gen. 21:8-21	86:1-10, 16-17	Rom. 6:1*b*-11	Matt. 10:24-39
RoCath	Jer. 20:10-13	69 (rel. vv. 8-10 14, 17, 33-35	Rom. 5:12-15	Matt. 10:26-33
Episcopal	Jer. 20:7-13	69:1-18	Rom. 5:15*b*-19	Matt. 10:(16-23) 24-33
Lutheran	Jer. 20:7-13	69:1-20	Rom. 5:12-15	Matt. 10:24-33
		PROPER 8 (June 26-July 2) [RoCath: 13th Ordinary Time] [Luth: 6th After Pentecost]		
RCL	Gen. 22:1-14	13	Rom. 6:12-23	Matt. 10:40-42
RoCath	II Kings 4:8-11, 14-16	89:2-3, 16-19	Rom. 6:3-4, 8-11	Matt. 10:37-42
Episcopal	Isa. 2:10-17	89:1-18	Rom 6:3-11	Matt. 10:34-42
Lutheran	Jer. 28:5-9	89:1-4, 15-18	Rom. 6:1*b*-11	Matt. 10:34-42

	Old Testament	Psalm	Epistle	Gospel
		PROPER 9 (July 3-9) [RoCath: 14th Ordinary Time] [Luth: 7th After Pentecost]		
RCL	Gen. 24:34-38, 42-49, 58-67	45:10-17	Rom. 7:15-25*a*	Matt. 11:16-19, 25-30
RoCath	Zech. 9:9-10	145:1-2, 8-11, 13-14	Rom 8:9, 11-13	Matt 11:25-30
Episcopal	Zech. 9:9-12	145	Rom. 7:21–8:6	Matt. 11:25-30
Lutheran	Zech. 9:9-12	145		Matt. 11:25-30
		PROPER 10 (July 10-16) [RoCath: 15th Ordinary Time] [Luth: 8th After Pentecost]		
RCL	Gen. 25:19-34	119:105-112	Rom. 8:1-11	Matt. 13:1-9, 18-23
RoCath	Isa. 55:10-11	65:10-14	Rom. 8:18-23	Matt. 13:1-23
Episcopal	Isa. 55:1-5, 10-13	65	Rom. 8:9-17	
Lutheran	Isa. 55:10-11		65	Rom. 8:18-25

	Old Testament	Psalm	Epistle	Gospel
		PROPER 11 (July 17-23) [RoCath: 16th Ordinary Time] [Luth: 9th After Pentecost]		
RCL	Gen. 28:10-19*a*	139:1-12, 23-34	Rom. 8:12-25	Matt. 13:24-30, 36-43
RoCath	Sir. 12:13, 16-19	86:5-6, 9-10, 15-16	Rom. 8:26-27	Matt. 13:24-43
Episcopal	Sir. 12:13, 16-19	86	Rom. 8:18-25	
Lutheran	Isa. 44:6-8	86:11-17	Rom. 8:26-27	
		PROPER 12 (July 24-30) [RoCath: 17th Ordinary Time] [Luth: 10th After Pentecost]		
RCL	Gen. 29:15-28	105:1-11, 45*b*	Rom. 8:26-39	Matt. 13:31-33, 44-52
Cte		or 128		
RoCath	I Kings 3:5, 7-12	119:57, 72, 76-77, 127-130	Rom. 8:28-30	Matt. 13:44-52
Episcopal	I Kings 3:5-12	119:121-136	Rom. 6:26-34	Matt. 13:31-33, 44-49*a*
Lutheran	I Kings 3:5-12	119:129-136	Rom. 8:28-30	Matt. 13:44-52

	Old Testament	Psalm	Epistle	Gospel
		PROPER 13 (July 31-August 6) [RoCath: 18th Ordinary Time] [Luth: 11th After Pentecost]		
RCL	Gen. 32:22-31	17:1-7, 15	Rom. 9:1-5	Matt. 14:13-21
RoCath	Isa. 55:1-3	145:8-9, 15-18	Rom. 8:35, 37-39	
Episcopal	Neh. 9:16-20	78:1-29	Rom. 8:35-39	
Lutheran	Isa. 55:1-5	104:25-31	Rom. 8:35-39	
		PROPER 14 (August 7-13) [RoCath: 19th Ordinary Time] [Luth: 12th After Pentecost]		
RCL	Gen. 37:1-4, 12-36	105:1-6, 16-22, 45*b*	Rom. 10:5-15	Matt. 14:22-33
RoCath	I Kings 19:9, 11-13	85:9-14	Rom. 9:1-5	
Episcopal	Jonah 2:1-9	29	Rom. 9:1-5	
Lutheran	I Kings 19:9-18	85:8-13	Rom. 9:1-5	

	Old Testament	Psalm	Epistle	Gospel
		PROPER 15 (August 14-20) [RoCath: 20th Ordinary Time] [Luth: 13th After Pentecost]		
RCL	Gen. 45:1-15	133	Rom. 11:1-2*a*, 29-32	Matt. 15:(10-20), 21-28
RoCath	Isa. 56:1, 6-7	67:2-3, 5, 6, 8	Rom. 11:13-15, 29-32	Matt. 15:21-28
Episcopal	Isa. 56:1 (2-5) 6-7	67	Rom. 11:13-15 29-32	Matt. 15:21-28
Lutheran	Isa. 56:1, 6-8	67	Rom. 11:13-15, 29-32	Matt. 15:21-28
		PROPER 16 (August 21-27) [RoCath: 21st Ordinary Time] [Luth: 14th After Pentecost]		
RCL	Exod. 1:8–2:10	124	Rom. 12:1-8	Matt. 16:13-20
RoCath	Isa. 22:15, 19-23	138:1-3, 6, 8	Rom. 11:33-36	
Episcopal	Isa. 51:1-6	138	Rom. 11:33-36	
Lutheran	Exod. 6:2-8	138	Rom. 11:33-36	

	Old Testament	Psalm	Epistle	Gospel
	PROPER 17 (August 28-September 3) [RoCath: 22nd Ordinary Time] [Luth: 15th After Pentecost]			
RCL	Exod. 3:1-15	105:1-6, 23-26, 45*c*	Rom. 12:9-21	Matt. 16:21-28
RoCath	Jer. 20:7-9	63:2-6, 8-9	Rom. 12:1-2	Matt. 16:21-27
Episcopal	Jer. 15:15-21	26	Rom. 12:1-8	Matt. 16:21-27
Lutheran	Jer. 15:15-21	26	Rom. 12:1-8	Matt. 16:21-26

A LITURGICAL CALENDAR: Trinity Sunday and Propers Four Through Seventeen 1992–2001

A Liturgical Calendar

Trinity Sunday Through August 1992–2001

	1993 A	1994 B	1995 C	1996 A	1997 B
Trinity	June 6	May 29	June 11	June 2	May 25
Proper 4	———	———	———	———	June 1
Proper 5	———	June 5	———	June 9	June 8
Proper 6	June 13	June 12	June 18	June 16	June 15
Proper 7	June 20	June 19	June 25	June 23	June 22
Proper 8	June 27	June 26	July 2	June 30	June 29
Proper 9	July 4	July 3	July 9	July 7	July 6
Proper 10	July 11	July 10	July 16	July 14	July 13
Proper 11	July 18	July 17	July 23	July 21	July 20
Proper 12	July 25	July 24	July 30	July 28	July 27
Proper 13	Aug. 1	July 31	Aug. 6	Aug. 4	Aug. 3
Proper 14	Aug. 8	Aug. 7	Aug. 13	Aug. 11	Aug. 10
Proper 15	Aug. 15	Aug. 14	Aug. 20	Aug. 18	Aug. 17
Proper 16	Aug. 22	Aug. 21	Aug. 27	Aug. 25	Aug. 24
Proper 17	Aug. 29	Aug. 28	Sept. 3	Sept. 1	Aug. 31

	1998 C	1999 A	2000 B	2001 C
Trinity	June 7	May 30	June 18	June 10
Proper 4	———	———	———	———
Proper 5	———	June 6	———	———
Proper 6	June 14	June 13	———	June 17
Proper 7	June 21	June 20	June 25	June 24
Proper 8	June 28	June 27	July 2	July 1
Proper 9	July 5	July 4	July 9	July 8
Proper 10	July 12	July 11	July 16	July 15
Proper 11	July 19	July 18	July 23	July 22
Proper 12	July 26	July 25	July 30	July 29
Proper 13	Aug. 2	Aug. 1	Aug. 6	Aug. 5
Proper 14	Aug. 9	Aug. 8	Aug. 13	Aug. 12
Proper 15	Aug. 16	Aug. 15	Aug. 20	Aug. 19
Proper 16	Aug. 23	Aug. 22	Aug. 27	Aug. 26
Proper 17	Aug. 30	Aug. 29	Sept. 3	Sept. 2